SIDE by SIDE

THIRD EDITION

BOOK 2A

Steven J. Molinsky
Bill Bliss

Illustrated by

Richard E. Hill

Longman

Side by Side, 3rd edition
Student Book/Activity Workook 2A

Pearson Education, 10 Bank Street, White Plains, NY 10606

Vice president, director of publishing: *Allen Ascher*
Editorial manager: *Pam Fishman*
Vice president, director of design and production: *Rhea Banker*
Associate director of electronic production: *Aliza Greenblatt*
Production manager: *Ray Keating*
Director of manufacturing: *Patrice Fraccio*
Digital layout specialist: *Wendy Wolf*
Associate art director: *Elizabeth Carlson*
Interior design: *Elizabeth Carlson, Wendy Wolf*
Cover design: *Elizabeth Carlson*
Copyediting: *Janet Johnston*

Contributing *Side by Side* Gazette authors: *Laura English, Meredith Westfall*

Photo credits: p. 27, (*left*) Fotolia.com, (*right*) Rudy Von Briel/PhotoEdit; p. 28 (*top*) Cosmo Condina/Stone, (*bottom*)
Eric Larrayadieu/Getty Images, (*center*) Don Smetzer/Stone; p. 59, (*top*) Courtesy Guinness World Records, Ltd.,
(*center, left*) Inacio Teixeira/AP/Wide World Photos, (*center, right*) Hugh Sitton/Stone, (*bottom, left*) Chad
Ehlers/Stone; p. 60, (*top*) Ray Stott/The Image Works, (*center*) Margot Granitsas/The Image Works, (*bottom*)
Popperfoto/Archive Photos.

The authors gratefully acknowledge the contribution
of Tina Carver in the development of the original
Side by Side program.

ISBN-10: 0-13-029301-6
ISBN-13: 978-0-13-029301-5

15 16 17 18 19 – V082 – 17 16 15 14 13

1

Review of Tenses:
Simple Present
Present Continuous
Simple Past
Future: Going to

Like to
Time Expressions
Indirect Object
Pronouns

- Describing Present, Past, and Future Actions
- Birthdays and Gifts
- Telling About Friendships

VOCABULARY PREVIEW

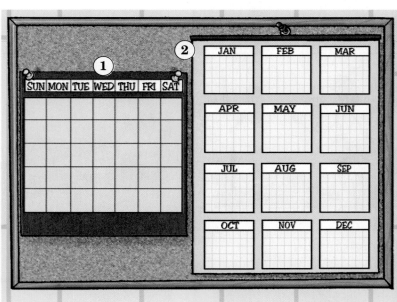

1. **Days of the Week**
   Sunday
   Monday
   Tuesday
   Wednesday
   Thursday
   Friday
   Saturday

2. **Months of the Year**
   January
   February
   March
   April
   May
   June
   July
   August
   September
   October
   November
   December

3. **Seasons**
   spring
   summer
   fall / autumn
   winter

What Do You Like to Do on the Weekend?

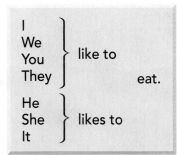

I We You They	like to
	eat.
He She It	likes to

A. What do you like to do on the weekend?

B. I like to read.

A. What does Ron like to do on the weekend?

B. He likes to go to the mall.

1. *Mr. and Mrs. Johnson?*
watch TV

2. *Tom?*
play basketball

3. *Sally?*
go to the beach

4. *you and your friends?*
chat online

5. *your grandmother?*
go hiking

6. *you?*

TALK ABOUT IT! *What Do They Like to Do?*

cook	play	swim	write
cooks	plays	swims	writes
cooked	played	swam	wrote
cooking	playing	swimming	writing

Robert likes to cook.
He cooks every day.
He cooked yesterday.
He's cooking right now.
He's going to cook tomorrow.
As you can see, Robert REALLY likes to cook.

Irene likes to play the piano.
She plays the piano every day.
She played the piano yesterday.
She's playing the piano right now.
She's going to play the piano tomorrow.
As you can see, Irene REALLY likes to play
     the piano.

Jimmy and Patty like to swim.*
They swim every day.
They swam yesterday.
They're swimming right now.
They're going to swim tomorrow.
As you can see, Jimmy and Patty REALLY
     like to swim.

Jonathan likes to write.
He writes every day.
He wrote yesterday.
He's writing right now.
He's going to write tomorrow.
As you can see, Jonathan REALLY likes to
     write.

Using these questions, talk about the people above with students in your class.

What does _____ like to do?
What does he/she do every day?
What did he/she do yesterday?
What's he/she doing right now?
What's he/she going to do tomorrow?

What do _____ like to do?
What do they do every day?
What did they do yesterday?
What are they doing right now?
What are they going to do tomorrow?

Then use these questions to talk about other people you know.

* swim – swam

Are You Going to Cook Spaghetti This Week?

Past Time Expressions

yesterday
yesterday morning/afternoon/evening
last night
last week/weekend/month/year

last Sunday/Monday/.../Saturday
last January/February/.../December
last spring/summer/fall (autumn)/winter

A. Are you going to cook spaghetti this week?

B. No, I'm not. I cooked spaghetti LAST week, and
I don't like to cook spaghetti very often.

1. Are you going to watch videos today?

2. Are you going to drive downtown this
weekend?

3. Is Mrs. Miller going to plant flowers
this spring?

4. Is your father going to make pancakes
this morning?

5. Are Mr. and Mrs. Jenkins going to the mall* this Saturday?

6. Are you and your friends going skiing this December?

7. Are you going to write letters tonight?

8. Is Dave going to clean his room this week?

9. Are you and your family going to WonderWorld this year?

10.

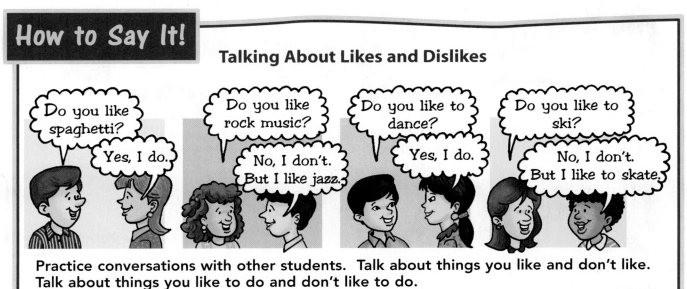

How to Say It!

Talking About Likes and Dislikes

Do you like spaghetti?

Yes, I do.

Do you like rock music?

No, I don't. But I like jazz.

Do you like to dance?

Yes, I do.

Do you like to ski?

No, I don't. But I like to skate.

Practice conversations with other students. Talk about things you like and don't like. Talk about things you like to do and don't like to do.

* going to the mall = going to go to the mall

5

What Are You Going to Give Your Wife?

I'm going to give { my husband / my wife } a present.   I'm going to give { him / her } a present.

A. What are you going to give your wife for her birthday?

B. I don't know. I can't give her a necklace. I gave her a necklace last year.

A. How about flowers?

B. No. I can't give her flowers. I gave her flowers two years ago.

A. Well, what are you going to give her?

B. I don't know. I really have to think about it.

A. What are you going to give your _____ for (his/her) birthday?

B. I don't know. I can't _____. I _____ last year.

A. How about _____?

B. No. I can't _____. I _____ two years ago.

A. Well, what are you going to give (him/her)?

B. I don't know. I really have to think about it.

1. *husband*
   a watch
   a briefcase

2. *girlfriend*
   perfume
   a bracelet

3. *boyfriend*
   a jacket
   a sweater

4. *grandmother*
   flowers
   candy

5. *daughter*
   a bicycle
   a doll

6.

What Did Your Parents Give You?

I	me
he	him
she	her
we	us
you	you
they	them

A. What did your parents give you for your birthday?

B. They gave me a CD player.

1. What did you give your parents for their anniversary?
a painting

2. What did Mr. Lee's grandchildren give him for his birthday?
a computer

3. What did your children give you and your wife for your anniversary?
a plant

4. I forget. What did you give me for my last birthday?
a purple blouse with pink polka dots

MAY 12

How to Read a Date

January 23rd = January twenty-third
November 16th = November sixteenth
December 31st = December thirty-first

A. When is your birthday?
B. My birthday is _____.

SIDE by SIDE JOURNAL

Write in your journal about your last birthday. What did you do on your birthday? Did your family or friends give you any presents? Write about it.

VERY GOOD FRIENDS: EAST AND WEST

Eric and Susan are very good friends. They grew up together, they went to high school together, and they went to college together. Now Eric lives in California, and Susan lives in New Jersey. Even though they live far apart, they're still very good friends.

They write to each other very often. He writes her letters about life on the West Coast, and she writes him letters about life on the East Coast. They never forget each other's birthday. Last year he sent* her some CDs, and she sent him a wallet. Eric and Susan help each other very often. Last year he lent* her money when she was in the hospital, and she gave him advice when he lost* his job.

Eric and Susan like each other very much. They were always very good friends, and they still are.

VERY GOOD FRIENDS: NORTH AND SOUTH

Carlos and Maria are our very good friends. For many years we went to church together, we took vacations together, and our children played together. Now Carlos and Maria live in Florida, and we still live here in Wisconsin. Even though we live far apart, we're still very good friends.

We communicate with each other very often on the Internet. We send them messages about life up north, and they send us messages about life down south. We never forget each others' anniversaries. Last year we sent them Wisconsin cheese, and they sent us Florida oranges. We also help each other very often. Last year we lent them money when they bought a new van, and they gave us advice when we sold* our house and moved into a condominium.

We like each other very much. We were always very good friends, and they still are.

* send – sent   lose – lost
   lend – lent   sell – sold

✔ READING *CHECK-UP*

TRUE OR FALSE?

1. Eric and Susan are in high school.
2. Eric lives on the West Coast.
3. Susan sent Eric some CDs last year.
4. Susan was sick last year.
5. They were friends when they were children.
6. Carlos and Maria don't live in Wisconsin now.
7. Florida is in the north.
8. Carlos and Maria send messages on the Internet.
9. Carlos and Maria moved into a condominium last year.

LISTENING

Listen and choose the correct answer.

1. a. I like to play tennis.
    b. I'm going to play tennis.
2. a. I went to the beach.
    b. I go to the beach.
3. a. Yesterday morning.
    b. Tomorrow afternoon.
4. a. I gave them a plant.
    b. I'm going to give them a plant.

5. a. We went to the mall.
    b. We're going to the mall.
6. a. They sent messages last week.
    b. They send messages every week.
7. a. He gave her flowers.
    b. She gave him flowers.
8. a. Last weekend.
    b. Tomorrow morning.

IN YOUR OWN WORDS

FOR WRITING AND DISCUSSION

A VERY GOOD FRIEND

Do you have a very good friend who lives far away? Tell about your friendship.

How do you know each other?
How do you communicate with each other?
   (Do you call? write? send e-mail messages?)
What do you talk about or write about?
Do you send each other presents?
Do you help each other? How?

PRONUNCIATION *Contrastive Stress*

Listen. Then say it.

I'm not going to clean my room this week.
I cleaned my room LÁST week.

I'm not going to make pancakes this morning.
I made pancakes YÉSTERDAY morning.

Say it. Then listen.

I'm not going to watch videos tonight.
I watched videos LÁST night.

I'm not going to write letters this evening.
I wrote letters YÉSTERDAY evening.

GRAMMAR

SIMPLE PRESENT TENSE

I We You They	cook.
He She It	cooks.

LIKE TO

I We You They	like to / don't like to	
He She It	likes to / doesn't like to	cook.

PRESENT CONTINUOUS TENSE

(I am)	I'm	
(He is) (She is) (It is)	He's She's It's	cooking.
(We are) (You are) (They are)	We're You're They're	

SIMPLE PAST TENSE

I He She It We You They	cooked.

FUTURE: GOING TO

I'm He's She's It's We're You're They're	going to cook.

Am	I	
Is	he she it	going to cook?
Are	we you they	

	I	am.
Yes,	he she it	is.
	we you they	are.

	I'm	not.
No,	he she it	isn't.
	we you they	aren't.

INDIRECT OBJECT PRONOUNS

He gave	me him her it us you them	a present.

PAST TIME EXPRESSIONS

yesterday
yesterday morning / afternoon / evening
last night
last week / weekend / month / year
last Sunday / Monday / . . . / Saturday
last January / February / . . . / December
last spring / summer / fall (autumn) / winter

IRREGULAR VERBS

drive – drove
give – gave
go – went
lend – lent
lose – lost
sell – sold
send – sent
swim – swam
write – wrote

KEY VOCABULARY

EVERYDAY ACTIVITIES

chat online
clean
cook
drive
go *hiking*
go to *the mall*
make *pancakes*
plant
play *basketball*
play the *piano*
read
swim
watch TV
write

DAYS OF THE WEEK

Sunday
Monday
Tuesday
Wednesday
Thursday
Friday
Saturday

MONTHS OF THE YEAR

January
February
March
April
May
June
July
August
September
October
November
December

SEASONS

spring
summer
fall / autumn
winter

Count/Non-Count Nouns

- **Food**
- **Buying Food**
- **Being a Guest at Mealtime**
- **Describing Food Preferences**

VOCABULARY PREVIEW

1. apples	7. chicken	13. lettuce	19. pears
2. bananas	8. eggs	14. mayonnaise	20. pepper
3. bread	9. fish	15. meat	21. potatoes
4. cake	10. grapes	16. mustard	22. salt
5. carrots	11. ketchup	17. onions	23. soy sauce
6. cheese	12. lemons	18. oranges	24. tomatoes

Practice conversations with other students. Talk about the foods in this kitchen.

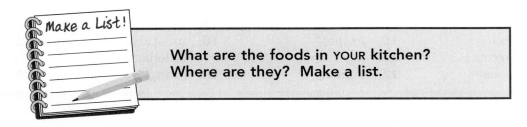

What are the foods in YOUR kitchen?
Where are they? Make a list.

Let's Make Sandwiches for Lunch!

1. Let's make pizza for lunch!
cheese

2. Let's make some fresh lemonade!
lemons

3. Let's make a salad for dinner!
lettuce

4. Let's make an omelet for breakfast!
eggs

5. Let's bake a cake for dessert!
flour

6. Let's make some fresh orange juice for breakfast!
oranges

7. Let's have french fries with our hamburgers!
potatoes

8. Let's have meatballs with our spaghetti!
meat

9.

How Much Milk Do You Want?

how much?	how many?
too much	too many
a little	a few

A. How much milk do you want?

B. Not too much. Just a little.

A. Okay. Here you are.

B. Thanks.

A. How many cookies do you want?

B. Not too many. Just a few.

A. Okay. Here you are.

B. Thanks.

1. *rice*

2. *french fries*

3. *ice cream*

4. *coffee*

5. *meatballs*

6.

Some of your friends are having dinner at your home. How do they like the food? Ask them.

A. How do you like the _____?

B. I think (it's / they're) delicious.

A. I'm glad you like (it / them). Would you care for some more?

B. Yes, please. But not (too much / too many). Just (a little / a few).
My doctor says that (too much / too many) _____ (is / are) bad for my health.

chocolate cake   *cookies*   *ice cream*

How to Say It!

Complimenting About Food

A. This *chicken* is delicious!*
B. I'm glad you like it.

A. These *potatoes* are delicious!*
B. I'm glad you like them.

* delicious / very good / excellent / wonderful / fantastic

Practice conversations with other students.

READING

TWO BAGS OF GROCERIES

Henry is at the supermarket, and he's really upset. He just bought some groceries, and he can't believe he just spent* sixty dollars! He bought only a few oranges, a few apples, a little milk, a little ice cream, and a few eggs.

He also bought just a little coffee, a few onions, a few bananas, a little rice, a little cheese, and a few lemons. He didn't buy very much fish, he didn't buy very many grapes, and he didn't buy very much meat.

Henry just spent sixty dollars, but he's walking out of the supermarket with only two bags of groceries. No wonder he's upset!

* spend – spent

✔ READING *CHECK-UP*

Q & A

Using these models, make questions and answers based on the story.

A. How many *oranges* did he buy?
B. He bought only a few *oranges*.

A. How much *milk* did he buy?
B. He bought only a little *milk*.

How About You?

What did YOU buy the last time you went to the supermarket?

I bought { a few . . .
         { a little . . .

LISTENING

Listen and choose what the people are talking about.

1. a. cake   b. carrots
2. a. fish   b. potatoes
3. a. cookies   b. milk
4. a. cheese   b. meatballs

5. a. eggs   b. butter
6. a. rice   b. french fries
7. a. oranges   b. salad
8. a. lemonade   b. lemons

DELICIOUS!

Lucy likes french fries. In fact, she eats them all the time. Her friends often tell her that she eats too many french fries, but Lucy doesn't think so. She thinks they're delicious.

Fred likes ice cream. In fact, he eats it all the time. His doctor often tells him that he eats too much ice cream, but Fred doesn't think so. He thinks it's delicious.

TASTES TERRIBLE!

Daniel doesn't like vegetables. In fact, he never eats them. His parents often tell him that vegetables are good for him, but Daniel doesn't care. He thinks they taste terrible.

Alice doesn't like yogurt. In fact, she never eats it. Her children often tell her that yogurt is good for her, but Alice doesn't care. She thinks it tastes terrible.

ON YOUR OWN

Tell about foods you like.

What foods do you think are delicious?
How often do you eat them?
Are they good for you, or are they bad for you?

Tell about foods you don't like.

What foods do you think taste terrible?
How often do you eat them?
Are they good for you, or are they bad for you?

Listen. Then say it.

Let's make a salad for dinner!

Let's make eggs for breakfast!

Would you care for some more cake?

It's bad for my health.

Say it. Then listen.

Let's make pizza for lunch!

Let's have ice cream for dessert!

Would you care for some more cookies?

They're bad for my health.

SIDE by SIDE JOURNAL

Write in your journal about your favorite foods. What are they? How often do you eat them? Why do you like them?

CHAPTER SUMMARY

GRAMMAR

COUNT / NON-COUNT NOUNS

There isn't any	bread. lettuce. flour.

There aren't any	apples. eggs. lemons.

How much	milk cheese ice cream	do you want?
How many	cookies french fries meatballs	

Not too	much.
	many.

Just	a little.
	a few.

KEY VOCABULARY

FOODS

apple pie	carrots	fish	ketchup	meatballs	oranges	salad	sugar
apples	cheese	flour	lemonade	milk	pears	salt	tea
bananas	chicken	french fries	lemons	mustard	pepper	sandwich	tomatoes
bread	coffee	grapes	lettuce	omelet	pizza	soda	vegetables
butter	cookies	hamburgers	mayonnaise	onions	potatoes	soy sauce	yogurt
cake	eggs	ice cream	meat	orange juice	rice	spaghetti	

Partitives
Count/Non-Count Nouns
Imperatives

- **Buying Food**
- **Describing Food**
- **Eating in a Restaurant**
- **Recipes**

VOCABULARY PREVIEW

1. a **can** of soup
2. a **jar** of jam
3. a **bottle** of ketchup
4. a **box** of cereal
5. a **bag** of flour
6. a **loaf** of white bread
7. two **loaves** of whole wheat bread
8. a **bunch** of bananas
9. a **head** of lettuce
10. a **dozen** eggs
11. a **pint** of ice cream
12. a **quart** of orange juice
13. a **gallon** of milk
14. a **pound** of meat
15. a **half pound** / **half a pound** } of cheese

Do We Need Anything from the Supermarket?

My Shopping List

a can of soup
a jar of jam
a bottle of ketchup
a box of cereal
a bag of flour
a loaf of white bread
2 loaves of whole wheat bread
a bunch of bananas
2 bunches of carrots

a head of lettuce
a dozen eggs

a pt.* of ice cream
a qt.* of orange juice
a gal.* of milk
a lb.* of meat
1/2 lb.* of cheese

* pt. = pint
  qt. = quart
  gal. = gallon
  lb. = pound

A. Do we need anything from the supermarket?

B. Yes. We need a loaf of bread.

A. A loaf of bread?

B. Yes.

A. Anything else?

B. No. Just a loaf of bread.

1.   2.   3.   4.   5.

6.   7.   8.   9.   10.

Make a Shopping List!

What do you need from the supermarket?
Make a shopping list.

How Much Does a Head of Lettuce Cost?

1¢	$.01	one cent	$1.00	one dollar
25¢	$.25	twenty-five cents	$10.00	ten dollars

A. How much does **a head of lettuce** cost?

B. **A dollar ninety-five.*** ($1.95)

A. A DOLLAR NINETY-FIVE?! That's a lot of money!

B. You're right. **Lettuce** is very expensive this week.

* $1.95 = { a dollar ninety-five
one dollar and ninety-five cents

A. How much does **a pound of apples** cost?

B. **Two eighty-nine.*** ($2.89)

A. TWO EIGHTY-NINE?! That's a lot of money!

B. You're right. **Apples** are very expensive this week.

* $2.89 = { two eighty-nine
two dollars and eighty-nine cents

1.

2.

3.

4.

5.

6.

7.

8.

READING

NOTHING TO EAT FOR DINNER

Joan got home late from work today, and she was very hungry. When she opened the refrigerator, she was upset. There was nothing to eat for dinner. Joan sat down and made a shopping list. She needed a head of lettuce, a bunch of carrots, a quart of milk, a dozen eggs, two pounds of tomatoes, half a pound of chicken, and a loaf of bread.

Joan rushed out of the house and drove to the supermarket. When she got there, she was very disappointed. There wasn't any lettuce. There weren't any carrots. There wasn't any milk. There weren't any eggs. There weren't any tomatoes. There wasn't any chicken, and there wasn't any bread.

Joan was tired and upset. In fact, she was so tired and upset that she lost her appetite, drove home, didn't have dinner, and went to bed.

✔ READING *CHECK-UP*

Q & A

Joan is at the supermarket. Using these models, create dialogs based on the story.

A. Excuse me. I'm looking for *a head of lettuce*.
B. Sorry. There isn't any more *lettuce*.
A. There isn't?
B. No, there isn't. Sorry.

A. Excuse me. I'm looking for *a bunch of carrots*.
B. Sorry. There aren't any more *carrots*.
A. There aren't?
B. No, there aren't. Sorry.

LISTENING

Listen and choose what the people are talking about.

1. a. chicken   b. milk
2. a. oranges   b. flour
3. a. cookies   b. bread
4. a. potatoes   b. lettuce
5. a. eggs   b. meat
6. a. cereal   b. bananas
7. a. cake   b. soup
8. a. onions   b. soda

What Would You Like?

A. What would you like **for dessert**?

B. I can't decide. What do you recommend?

A. I recommend our **chocolate ice cream**. Everybody says **it's** delicious.*

B. Okay. Please give me **a dish of chocolate ice cream**.

A. What would you like **for breakfast**?

B. I can't decide. What do you recommend?

A. I recommend our **scrambled eggs**. Everybody says **they're** out of this world.*

B. Okay. Please give me **an order of scrambled eggs**.

* delicious / very good / excellent / wonderful / fantastic / magnificent / out of this world

1. for lunch?
   a bowl of

2. for breakfast?
   an order of

3. for dessert?
   a piece of

4. to drink?
   a glass of

5. for dessert?
   a bowl of

6. to drink?
   a cup of

7. for dessert?
   a dish of

8.

How to Say It!

Making a Recommendation About Food

A. What do you recommend for *breakfast*?*

B. I { recommend / suggest } the *pancakes*.

* breakfast / lunch / dinner / dessert

Practice conversations with other students. Ask for and make recommendations.

Stanley's Favorite Recipes

Are you going to have a party soon? Do you want to cook something special? Stanley the chef recommends this recipe for VEGETABLE STEW. Everybody says it's fantastic!

1. Put **a little butter** into a saucepan.

2. Chop up **a few onions**.

3. Cut up (**a little / a few**) _____.

4. Pour in _____.

5. Slice _____.

6. Add _____.

7. Chop up _____.

8. Slice _____.

9. Add _____.

10. Cook for 3 hours.

When is your English teacher's birthday? Do you want to bake a special cake? Stanley the chef recommends this recipe for FRUITCAKE. Everybody says it's out of this world!

1. Put **a few cups of flour** into a mixing bowl.

2. Add **a little sugar**.

3. Slice (**a little / a few**) _____.

4. Cut up _____.

5. Pour in _____.

6. Add _____.

7. Chop up _____.

8. Add _____.

9. Mix in _____.

10. Bake for 45 minutes.

Project

Do you have a favorite recipe? Write the recipe, and share it with other students. Then as a class, put all your recipes together and make a class cookbook.

READING

AT THE CONTINENTAL RESTAURANT

Yesterday was Sherman and Dorothy Johnson's thirty-fifth wedding anniversary. They went to the Continental Restaurant for dinner. This restaurant is a very special place for Sherman and Dorothy because they went there on their first date thirty-six years ago.

Sherman and Dorothy sat at a quiet romantic table in the corner. They looked at the menu, and then they ordered dinner. For an appetizer, Dorothy ordered a bowl of vegetable soup, and Sherman ordered a glass of tomato juice. For the main course, Dorothy ordered baked chicken with rice, and Sherman ordered broiled fish with potatoes. For dessert, Dorothy ordered a piece of apple pie, and Sherman ordered a bowl of strawberries.

Sherman and Dorothy enjoyed their dinner very much. The soup was delicious, and the tomato juice was fresh. The chicken was wonderful, and the rice was tasty. The fish was fantastic, and the potatoes were excellent. The apple pie was magnificent, and the strawberries were out of this world.

Sherman and Dorothy had a wonderful evening at the Continental Restaurant. It was a very special anniversary.

ROLE PLAY

Sherman and Dorothy are ordering dinner from their waiter or waitress. Using these lines to begin, work in groups of three and create a role play based on the story.

A. Would you like to order now?
B. Yes. For an appetizer, I'd like . . .
C. And I'd like . . .

Now, the waiter or waitress is asking about the dinner. Using this model, continue your role play based on all the foods in the story.

A. How (is / are) the _____?
B. (It's / They're) _____.
A. I'm glad you like (it / them).
And how (is / are) the _____?
C. (It's / They're) _____.
A. I'm glad you like (it / them).

PRONUNCIATION *Of* Before Consonants and Vowels

Listen. Then say it.

a bowl of soup

a head of lettuce

a piece of apple pie

a bag of onions

Say it. Then listen.

a glass of milk

a jar of jam

a pound of oranges

a dish of ice cream

In your journal, write about a special meal you enjoyed—in your home, in someone else's home, or at a restaurant. What foods did you have? Who was at the meal? Why was it special?

CHAPTER SUMMARY

GRAMMAR

COUNT / NON-COUNT NOUNS

Lettuce Butter Milk	is	very expensive.
Apples Carrots Onions	are	

Add	a little	salt. sugar. honey.
	a few	potatoes. nuts. raisins.

I recommend our	chocolate ice cream. scrambled eggs.

It's They're	delicious.

IMPERATIVES

Please **give me** a dish of ice cream.
Put a little butter into a saucepan.
Cook for 3 hours.

PARTITIVES

a **bag of** flour	a **dozen** eggs	a **jar of** jam	a **bowl of** chicken soup
a **bottle of** ketchup	a **gallon of** milk	a **loaf of** bread	a **cup of** hot chocolate
a **box of** cereal	a **half pound (half a pound) of** cheese	a **pint of** ice cream	a **dish of** ice cream
a **bunch of** bananas		a **pound of** meat	a **glass of** milk
a **can of** soup	a **head of** lettuce	a **quart of** orange juice	an **order of** scrambled eggs
			a **piece of** apple pie

KEY VOCABULARY

FOOD ITEMS

apple pie	hot chocolate	scrambled eggs	tomato juice	
baked chicken	jam	soup	vanilla ice cream	
baking soda	mushrooms	chicken soup	water	
broiled fish	nuts	vegetable soup	white bread	
chocolate ice cream	pancakes	strawberries	whole wheat bread	
honey	raisins	Swiss cheese		

DESCRIBING FOOD

delicious
excellent
fantastic
magnificent
out of this world
very good
wonderful

Volume 2   Number 1

Food Shopping

Everybody eats, and everybody shops for food!

In the past, people shopped for fruits, vegetables, bread, and meat at small food stores and at open markets. Before there were refrigerators, it was difficult to keep food fresh for a long time, so people shopped almost every day.

Life today is very different from the past. Refrigerators keep food fresh so people don't have to shop every day. People also have very busy lives. They have time to shop for food only once or twice a week.

People shop for food in different kinds of places—in small grocery stores, at large supermarkets, and sometimes at enormous wholesale stores that sell food and other items at very low prices. Some people even shop on the Internet. They order food online, and the company delivers it to their home. And in many places around the world, people still shop in little food stores and at open markets. There are certainly many different ways to shop for food these days!

FACT FILE

One Day's Food

Eggs: The world's hens produce more than 2 billion eggs a day—enough eggs to make an omelet the size of the island of Cyprus!

Chocolate: The world produces 8,818 tons of cocoa beans every day—enough to make 700 million chocolate bars!

Rice: The world produces 1.6 million tons of rice every day—an amount the size of Egypt's Great Pyramid!

I'd like _____ , please.

 ■ a hamburger

 ■ a hot dog

 ■ a sandwich

 ■ a taco

 ■ a bowl of chili

 ■ a slice of pizza

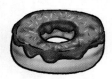 ■ a donut

 ■ a bagel

 ■ a muffin

AROUND THE WORLD

Where People Shop for Food

People in different places shop for food in different ways.

These people shop for food at an open market.

This person buys a fresh loaf of bread every day at this bakery.

These people go to a big supermarket once a week.

Where do people shop for food in countries you know? Where do YOU shop for food?

Global Exchange

Glen25: Hi, Maria. How are you today? I just had breakfast. I had a glass of orange juice, a bowl of cereal, and a muffin. At 12 noon I'm going to have lunch. For lunch I usually have a sandwich and a glass of milk. Our family's big meal of the day is dinner. We usually eat at about 6 P.M. We usually have meat, chicken, or fish, rice or potatoes, and vegetables. How about you? When do you usually eat? What do you have? What's your big meal of the day?

MariaV: Hi, Glen. It's the middle of the afternoon here. Our family just had our big meal of the day. Today we had meat, potatoes, and vegetables. For breakfast I usually have a roll and a cup of hot chocolate. We don't have a big dinner in the evening. We usually have a snack early in the evening and a light supper at about 9:30.

Send a message to a keypal. Tell about the meals you eat.

LISTENING

Attention, Food Shoppers!

_d_	**1** cereal	**a.**	$2.75
___	**2** bread	**b.**	$ .40
___	**3** orange juice	**c.**	$3.25
___	**4** ice cream	**d.**	$3.49
___	**5** bananas	**e.**	$1.79

What Are They Saying?

Future Tense: Will
Time Expressions
Might

- **Telling About the Future**
- **Probability**
- **Possibility**
- **Warnings**

VOCABULARY PREVIEW

1. begin
2. end
3. arrive
4. return
5. grow up
6. get married
7. name
8. move
9. helmet
10. safety glasses
11. warning

Will the Train Arrive Soon?

(I will)	I'll
(He will)	He'll
(She will)	She'll
(It will)	It'll } work.
(We will)	We'll
(You will)	You'll
(They will)	They'll

Will he work?
Yes, he will.

A. Will the train arrive soon?

B. Yes, it will. It'll arrive in five minutes.

1. Will the game begin soon?
at 7:00

2. Will Ms. Lopez return soon?
in an hour

3. Will you be ready soon?
in a few minutes

4. Will the guests be here soon?
in half an hour

5. Will your brother get home soon?
in a little while

6. Will you be back soon?
in a week

7. Will the storm end soon?
in a few hours

8. Will I get out of the hospital soon?
in two or three days

What Do You Think?

| I He She It We You They | will work. |

| I He She It We You They | won't work.
(will not) |

Do you think it'll rain tomorrow?

Maybe it will, and maybe it won't. We'll just have to wait and see.

1. Do you think Mr. Lee will give us a test tomorrow?

2. Do you think your daughter will get married soon?

3. Do you think your parents will move to Florida?

4. Do you think it'll be very cold this winter?

5. Do you think we'll have to work this weekend?

6. Do you think you'll be happy in your new neighborhood?

7. Do you think I'll be famous some day?

8. Do you think there will be many people at the beach tomorrow?

9. Do you think _____ ?

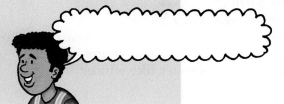

I CAN'T WAIT FOR SPRING TO COME!

I'm tired of winter. I'm tired of snow, I'm tired of cold weather, and I'm sick and tired of winter coats and boots! Just think! In a few more weeks it won't be winter any more. It'll be spring. The weather won't be cold. It'll be warm. It won't snow any more. It'll be sunny. I won't have to stay indoors any more. I'll go outside and play with my friends. We'll ride bicycles and play baseball again.

In a few more weeks our neighborhood won't look sad and gray any more. The flowers will bloom, and the trees will become green again. My family will spend more time outdoors. My father will work in the yard. He'll cut the grass and paint the fence. My mother will work in the yard, too. She'll buy new flowers and plant them in the garden. On weekends we won't just sit in the living room and watch TV. We'll go for walks in the park, and we'll have picnics on Sunday afternoons.

I can't wait for spring to come! Hurry, spring!

✔ **READING** *CHECK-UP*

TRUE, FALSE, OR MAYBE?

Answer True, False, or Maybe (if the answer isn't in the story).

1. It's spring.
2. The boy in the story likes to go outside during the spring.
3. The boy has a cold.
4. The trees are green now.
5. The park is near their house.
6. The boy plays baseball with his friends all year.
7. The family has a TV in their living room.
8. The boy's family doesn't like winter.

How About You?

What's your favorite season—spring? summer? fall? winter? Why? What's the weather like in your favorite season? What do you like to do?

They Really Can't Decide

| I He She It We You They | might clean it today. |

A. When are you going to clean your apartment?

B. I don't know. I might clean it today, or I might clean it next Saturday. I really can't decide.

A. Where are you going to go for your vacation?

B. We don't know. We might go to Mexico, or we might go to Japan. We really can't decide.

1. What's he going to make for dinner tonight?

2. What color is she going to paint her bedroom?

3. What are they going to name their new daughter?

4. When are you two going to get married?

5. What are you going to buy your brother for his birthday?

6. What are they going to do tonight?

7. How are you going to get to school tomorrow?

8. What's he going to name his new puppy?

9. What are you going to be when you grow up?

Careful!

A. Careful! Put on your helmet!

B. I'm sorry. What did you say?

A. Put on your helmet! You might hurt your head.

B. Oh. Thanks for the warning.

1. Put on your safety glasses!
   hurt your eyes

2. Don't stand there!
   get hit

3. Watch your step!
   fall

4. Don't touch that machine!
   get hurt

5. Don't touch those wires!
   get a shock

6.

How to Say It!

Asking for Repetition

A. *Careful! Watch your step!*

B. *I'm sorry.* { What did you say?
   Could you please repeat that?
   Could you say that again? }

Practice some conversations on this page again. Ask for repetition in different ways.

I'm Afraid I Might Drown

A. Would you like to go swimming with me?

B. No, I don't think so.

A. Why not?

B. I'm afraid I might drown.

A. Don't worry! You won't drown.

B. Are you sure?

A. I'm positive!

B. Okay. I'll go swimming with you.

1. *go skiing*
   break my leg

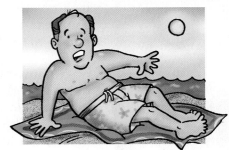

2. *go to the beach*
   get a sunburn

3. *go dancing*
   step on your feet

4. *take a walk in the park*
   catch a cold

5. *go to the movies*
   fall asleep

6. *go to the company picnic*
   have a terrible time

7. *go on the roller coaster*
   get sick

8. *go sailing*
   get seasick

9.

JUST IN CASE

Larry didn't go to work today, and he might not go to work tomorrow either. He might see his doctor instead. He's feeling absolutely terrible, and he thinks he might have the flu. Larry isn't positive, but he doesn't want to take any chances. He thinks it might be a good idea for him to see his doctor . . . just in case.

Mrs. Randall didn't go to the office today, and she might not go to the office tomorrow either. She might go to the doctor instead. She feels nauseous every morning, and she thinks she might be pregnant. Mrs. Randall isn't positive, but she doesn't want to take any chances. She thinks it might be a good idea for her to go to the doctor . . . just in case.

Tommy and Julie Harris didn't go to school today, and they might not go to school tomorrow either. They might stay home in bed instead. They have little red spots all over their arms and legs. Mr. and Mrs. Harris think their children might have the measles. They aren't positive, but they don't want to take any chances. They think it might be a good idea for Tommy and Julie to stay home in bed . . . just in case.

✔ READING *CHECK-UP*

CHOOSE

Larry is "calling in sick." Choose the correct words and then practice the conversation.

A. Hello. This is Larry Parker. I'm afraid I (might   can't)[1] come to work today. I think I (will   might)[2] have the flu.

B. That's too bad. (Are you   Will you)[3] going to see your doctor?

A. I think I (might   sure).[4]

B. (Not   Will)[5] you be at work tomorrow?

A. I'm not sure. I (might not   might)[6] go to work tomorrow either.

B. Well, I hope you feel better soon.

A. Thank you.

LISTENING

WHAT'S THE LINE?

Mrs. Harris (from the story on page 36) is calling Tommy and Julie's school. Listen and choose the correct lines.

1. a. Hello. This is Mrs. Harris.
   b. Hello. This is the Park Elementary School.
2. a. I can't.
   b. Tommy and Julie won't be in school today.
3. a. They might have the measles.
   b. Yes. This is their mother.
4. a. They aren't bad.   They're just sick.
   b. Yes.
5. a. Thank you.
   b. It might be a good idea.

Good morning. Park Elementary School.

WHAT'S THE WORD?

Listen and choose the word you hear.

1. a. can't   b. might
2. a. want to   b. won't
3. a. here   b. there
4. a. we'll   b. will
5. a. they'll   b. they
6. a. hurt   b. hit
7. a. I   b. I'll
8. a. red   b. wet
9. a. sick   b. seasick

Write a Note!

Your child didn't go to school yesterday. Write a note to the teacher and explain why.

..............., 20.......

Dear ....,

.... didn't go to school yesterday because

....

....

Sincerely,

....

PRONUNCIATION *Going to*

going to = gonna

Listen. Then say it.

When are you going to
   clean your room?
What color is she going to
   paint her bedroom?
How are they going to get
   to school?

Say it. Then listen.

When are you going to
   get married?
What's he going to name
   his cat?
When am I going to get
   out of the hospital?

SIDE by SIDE JOURNAL

Write in your journal about your future. Where do you think you might live? Where do you think you might work? What do you think might happen in your life?

CHAPTER SUMMARY

GRAMMAR

FUTURE TENSE: WILL

(I will)	I'll	
(He will)	He'll	
(She will)	She'll	
(It will)	It'll	work.
(We will)	We'll	
(You will)	You'll	
(They will)	They'll	

I	
He	
She	
It	won't work.
We	
You	
They	

Will	I he she it we you they	arrive soon?

Yes,	I he she it we you they	will.

No,	I he she it we you they	won't.

TIME EXPRESSIONS

The train will arrive	in	a few	days. minutes. hours. weeks. months.
		a week. an hour. half an hour. a little while. two or three days.	
	at seven o'clock.		

MIGHT

I He She It We You They	might clean it today.

KEY VOCABULARY

BEGINNINGS & ENDINGS	HEALTH	INJURIES	LIFE EVENTS
arrive	catch a cold	break *my* leg	get married
be back	get a sunburn	fall	grow up
begin	get seasick	get a shock	move
end	get sick	get hit	name (v)
get home		get hurt	
return	the flu	hurt *your* head/eyes	
	the measles		

38

Comparatives
Should
Possessive Pronouns

- **Making Comparisons**
- **Advice**
- **Expressing Opinions**
- **Agreement and Disagreement**

VOCABULARY PREVIEW

1. cute	6. hospitable	11. polite
2. delicious	7. hot / spicy	12. powerful
3. exciting	8. intelligent / smart	13. soft
4. fashionable	9. lazy	14. talented
5. friendly	10. light	15. talkative

My New Bicycle Is Faster

soft – softer small – smaller	large – larger safe – safer	big – bigger hot – hotter	fancy – fancier pretty – prettier

A. I think you'll like my new bicycle.

B. But I liked your OLD bicycle. It was **fast**.

A. That's right. But my new bicycle is **faster**.

1. *rug*
   soft

2. *tennis racket*
   light

3. *apartment*
   large

4. *neighborhood*
   safe

5. *office*
   big

6. *recipe for chili*
   hot

7. *dog*
   friendly

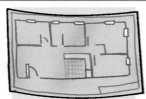

8. *sports car*
   fancy

9. *dishwasher*
   quiet

10. *wig*
    pretty

11. *cell phone*
    small

12. *cat*
    cute

My New Rocking Chair Is More Comfortable

fast – faster nice – nicer big – bigger pretty – prettier	comfortable – more comfortable beautiful – more beautiful interesting – more interesting intelligent – more intelligent

A. I think you'll like my new rocking chair.

B. But I liked your OLD rocking chair. It was **comfortable**.

A. That's right. But my new rocking chair is **more comfortable**.

1. *apartment building*
   beautiful

2. *roommate*
   interesting

3. *girlfriend*
   intelligent

4. *boyfriend*
   handsome

5. *briefcase*
   attractive

6. *computer*
   powerful

7. *printer*
   fast

8. *English teacher*
   smart

9. *recipe for meatloaf*
   delicious

10. *boss*
   nice

11. *parrot*
   talkative

12.

41

Bicycles Are Safer Than Motorcycles

I	
He	
She	
It	should study.
We	
You	
They	

Should I study?

safe

useful

A. Should I buy a bicycle or a motorcycle?

B. I think you should buy a bicycle.

A. Why?

B. Bicycles are **safer than** motorcycles.

A. Should he study English or Latin?

B. I think he should study English.

A. Why?

B. English is **more useful than** Latin.

cheap

1. Should I buy a used car or a new car?

Ellen interesting   Helen

2. Should he go out with Ellen or Helen?

friendly

3. Should she buy a dog or a cat?

honest

4. Should I vote for Linda Lee or Gary Green?

5. Should she take a course with Professor Blake or Professor Drake?

6. Should they plant flowers or vegetables this spring?

7. Should we buy this fan or that fan?

8. Should she buy these earrings or those earrings?

9. Should he take piano lessons with Mrs. Clark or Miss Smith?

10. Should I buy the hat in my left hand or the hat in my right hand?

11. Should she buy fur gloves or leather gloves?

12. Should I buy a notebook computer or a desktop computer?

13. Should I hire Ms. Parker or Ms. Jones?

14. Should I fire Mr. Mason or Mr. Grimes?

15. Should we rent this movie or that movie?

16.

READING

IT ISN'T EASY BEING A TEENAGER

I try to be a good son, but no matter how hard I try, my parents never seem to be satisfied. They think I should be a better* son. They think I should eat healthier food, I should wear nicer clothes, and I should get better grades. And according to them, my hair should be shorter, my room should be neater, and my friends should be more polite when they come to visit.

You know . . . it isn't easy being a teenager.

IT ISN'T EASY BEING PARENTS

We try to be good parents, but no matter how hard we try, our children never seem to be satisfied. They think we should be better parents. They think we should wear more fashionable clothes, we should drive a newer car, and we should listen to more interesting music. And according to them, we should be more sympathetic when they talk about their problems, we should be friendlier when their friends come to visit, and we should be more understanding when they come home late on Saturday night.

You know . . . it isn't easy being parents.

* good – better

✔ READING CHECK-UP

WHAT'S THE WORD?

According to this boy's parents, he doesn't eat healthy ¹ food, he doesn't wear _____² clothes, he doesn't get _____³ grades, his hair isn't _____⁴, and his friends aren't _____⁵ when they come to visit.

According to their children, these parents don't wear _____⁶ clothes, they don't have a _____⁷ car, they don't listen to _____⁸ music, and they aren't _____⁹ when their children's friends come to visit.

LISTENING

Listen and choose what the people are talking about.

1. a. TV   b. printer
2. a. chair   b. recipe
3. a. hair   b. apartment
4. a. offices   b. friends
5. a. neighborhood   b. briefcase
6. a. rug   b. computer

Don't Be Ridiculous!

my – mine	our – ours
his – his	your – yours
her – hers	their – theirs

A. You know, my dog isn't as friendly as your dog.

B. Don't be ridiculous! Yours is MUCH friendlier than **mine**.

A. You know, my novels aren't as interesting as Ernest Hemingway's novels.

B. Don't be ridiculous! Yours are MUCH more interesting than **his**.

clean

1. *my apartment*
your apartment

powerful

2. *my computer*
Bob's computer

nice

3. *my boss*
your boss

comfortable

4. *my furniture*
your furniture

big

5. *my house*
the Jacksons' house

She sells sea shells...
good

6. *my pronunciation*
Maria's pronunciation

pretty

7. *my garden*
your garden

delicious

8. *my recipe for fruitcake*
Stanley's recipe for fruitcake

9.

BROWNSVILLE

The Taylor family lived in Brownsville for many years. And for many years, Brownsville was a very good place to live. The streets were clean, the parks were safe, the bus system was reliable, and the schools were good.

But Brownsville changed. Today the streets aren't as clean as they used to be. The parks aren't as safe as they used to be. The bus system isn't as reliable as it used to be. And the schools aren't as good as they used to be.

Because of the changes in Brownsville, the Taylor family moved to Newport last year. In Newport the streets are cleaner, the parks are safer, the bus system is more reliable, and the schools are better. The Taylors are happy in Newport, but they were happier in Brownsville. Although Newport has cleaner streets, safer parks, a more reliable bus system, and better schools, Brownsville has friendlier people. They're nicer, more polite, and more hospitable than the people in Newport.

The Taylors miss Brownsville. Even though they're now living in Newport, Brownsville will always be their real home.

✔ READING *CHECK-UP*

Q & A

The people of Brownsville are calling Mayor Brown's radio talk show. They're upset about Brownsville's streets, parks, bus system, and schools. Using this model and the story, call Mayor Brown.

A. This is Mayor Brown. You're on the air.
B. Mayor Brown, I'm very upset about the *streets* here in Brownsville.
A. Why do you say that?
B. *They aren't* as *clean* as *they* used to be.
A. Do you really think so?
B. Definitely! You know . . . they say the *streets* in Newport *are cleaner*.
A. I'll see what I can do. Thank you for calling.

How to Say It!

Agreeing & Disagreeing

A. { I think . . .
    { In my opinion, . . .

B. { I agree.
    { I agree with you.
    { I think so, too.

C. { I disagree.
    { I disagree with you.
    { I don't think so.

Practice interactions on this page, using these expressions for agreeing and disagreeing.

INTERACTIONS

_____er
more _____ } than

as _____ as
not as _____ as

> I think New York is more interesting than Los Angeles.

> I disagree. I think Los Angeles is MUCH more interesting than New York.

> In my opinion, the weather in Honolulu is better than the weather in Miami.

> I don't think so. I think the weather in Miami is better than the weather in Honolulu.

> In my opinion, the people in Centerville aren't as friendly as the people in Greenville.

> I agree. But the people in Centerville are more interesting.

> I think so, too.

Practice conversations with other students. Compare different places you know.
Talk about . . .

the streets (_quiet, safe, clean, wide, busy_)
the buildings (_tall, modern, attractive_)
the weather (_cold, cool, warm, hot, rainy, snowy_)
the people (_friendly, nice, polite, honest, happy, hospitable, talkative, healthy_)
the city in general (_large, interesting, exciting, expensive_)

PRONUNCIATION Yes / No Questions with *or*

Listen. Then say it.

Should I buy a bicycle or a motorcycle?

Should we buy this fan or that fan?

Should he go out with Ellen or Helen?

Should she buy fur gloves or leather gloves?

Say it. Then listen.

Should they plant flowers or vegetables?

Should she buy these earrings or those earrings?

Should I hire Ms. Carter or Mr. Price?

Should I buy a notebook computer or a desktop computer?

SIDE by SIDE JOURNAL

In your journal, compare your home town and the place you live now. Or compare any two places you know.

CHAPTER SUMMARY

GRAMMAR

COMPARATIVES

My new apartment is	colder larger bigger prettier	than my old apartment.
	more comfortable more attractive	

SHOULD

Should	I he she it we you they	study?

I He She It We You They	should study.

POSSESSIVE PRONOUNS

This dog is much friendlier than	mine. his. hers. ours. yours. theirs.

KEY VOCABULARY

DESCRIBING

attractive	comfortable	fashionable	hospitable	neat	reliable	sympathetic
beautiful	convenient	fast	hot	new	safe	talented
big	cool	friendly	intelligent	nice	short	talkative
busy	cute	good–better	interesting	polite	small	tall
capable	delicious	handsome	large	powerful	smart	understanding
cheap	exciting	happy	lazy	pretty	snowy	useful
clean	expensive	healthy	light	quiet	soft	warm
cold	fancy	honest	modern	rainy	spicy	wide

6

Superlatives

- **Describing People, Places, and Things**
- **Shopping in a Department Store**
- **Expressing Opinions**

VOCABULARY PREVIEW

1. energetic	6. lazy	11. patient
2. funny	7. mean	12. popular
3. generous	8. nice	13. rude
4. helpful	9. noisy	14. sloppy
5. honest	10. obnoxious	15. stubborn

The Smartest Person I Know

smart – the smartest kind – the kindest	nice – the nicest safe – the safest
funny – the funniest pretty – the prettiest	big – the biggest hot – the hottest

A. I think your friend Margaret is very **smart**.

B. She certainly is. She's **the smartest** person I know.

1. *your Aunt Emma*
kind

2. *your friend Jim*
bright

3. *your parents*
nice

4. *your Uncle Ted*
funny

5. *your sister*
pretty

6. *your cousin Amy*
friendly

7. *Larry*
lazy

8. *your landlord*
mean

9. *your roommates*
sloppy

The Most Energetic Person I Know

smart – the smartest funny – the funniest nice – the nicest big – the biggest	energetic – the most energetic interesting – the most interesting patient – the most patient stubborn – the most stubborn

A. I think your grandmother is very **energetic**.

B. She certainly is. She's **the most energetic** person I know.

1. *your friend Carlos interesting*

2. *your grandfather generous*

3. *your cousins talented*

4. *our English teacher patient*

5. *your nephew Andrew stubborn*

6. *your younger brother polite*

7. *your older sister bright*

8. *your upstairs neighbor noisy*

9. *your downstairs neighbor rude*

10. *Senator Smith honest*

11. *our history professor boring*

12.

THE NICEST PERSON

friendly · polite · smart · talented · pretty

Mr. and Mrs. Jackson are very proud of their daughter, Linda. She's a very nice person. She's friendly, she's polite, she's smart, and she's talented. She's also very pretty.

Mr. and Mrs. Jackson's friends and neighbors always compliment them about Linda. They say she's the nicest person they know. According to them, she's the friendliest, the most polite, the smartest, and the most talented girl in the neighborhood. They also think she's the prettiest.

Mr. and Mrs. Jackson agree. They think Linda is a wonderful girl, and they're proud to say she's their daughter.

THE MOST OBNOXIOUS DOG

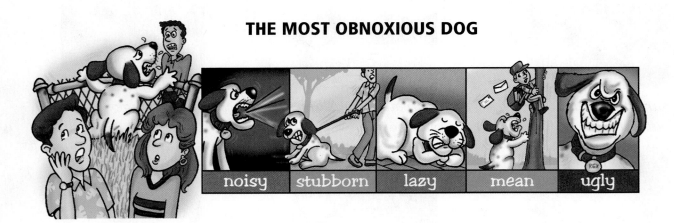

noisy · stubborn · lazy · mean · ugly

Mr. and Mrs. Hubbard are very embarrassed by their dog, Rex. He's a very obnoxious dog. He's noisy, he's stubborn, he's lazy, and he's mean. He's also very ugly.

Mr. and Mrs. Hubbard's friends and neighbors always complain about Rex. They say he's the most obnoxious dog they know. According to them, he's the noisiest, the most stubborn, the laziest, and the meanest dog in the neighborhood. They also think he's the ugliest.

Mr. and Mrs. Hubbard agree. They think Rex is a horrible dog, and they're ashamed to say he's theirs.

✓ READING CHECK-UP

CHOOSE

1. Linda is the (most polite   smart) person I know.
2. She's the most (talented   friendliest) girl in the neighborhood.
3. She's a very (nicest   nice) person.
4. Rex is the most (stubborn   mean) dog in the neighborhood.
5. He's the (lazy   noisiest) dog I know.
6. He's also the most (ugliest   obnoxious) dog in town.

Q & A

The neighbors are talking. Using these models, create dialogs based on the stories.

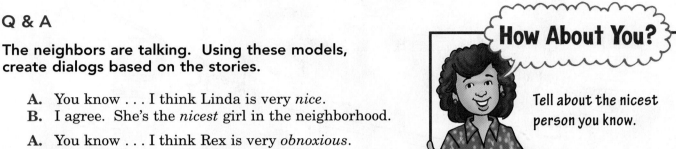

A. You know . . . I think Linda is very *nice*.
B. I agree. She's the *nicest* girl in the neighborhood.

A. You know . . . I think Rex is very *obnoxious*.
B. You're right. He's the *most obnoxious* dog in the neighborhood.

How About You?

Tell about the nicest person you know.

How to Say It!

Expressing an Opinion

A. { In my opinion, . . .
     As far as I'm concerned, . . .
     If you ask me, . . . } *Linda is the most talented student in our school.*

B. I agree. / I disagree.

Practice conversations with other students. Share opinions.

LISTENING

Listen to the sentence. Is the person saying something good or something bad about someone else?

1. a. good   b. bad
2. a. good   b. bad
3. a. good   b. bad
4. a. good   b. bad
5. a. good   b. bad
6. a. good   b. bad
7. a. good   b. bad
8. a. good   b. bad
9. a. good   b. bad

PRONUNCIATION *Linking Words with Duplicated Consonants*

Listen. Then say it.

She's the nicest teacher in our school.

He's the most stubborn neighbor on our street.

They're the most talented dancers in the world.

Say it. Then listen.

He's the most generous student in our class.

This is the cheapest toothpaste in the store.

He's the most polite taxi driver in the city.

I Want to Buy a Small Radio

a small radio	a comfortable chair	a good car
a smaller radio	a more comfortable chair	a better car
the smallest radio	the most comfortable chair	the best car

A. May I help you?

B. Yes, please. I want to buy a **small** radio.

A. I think you'll like this one. It's VERY **small**.

B. Don't you have a **smaller** one?

A. No, I'm afraid not. This is **the smallest** one we have.

B. Thank you anyway.

A. Sorry we can't help you. Please come again.

A. May I help you?

B. Yes, please. I want to buy a/an _____ _____.

A. I think you'll like this one. It's VERY _____.

B. Don't you have a/an { _____er / more _____ } one?

A. No, I'm afraid not. This is the { _____est / most _____ } one we have.

B. Thank you anyway.

A. Sorry we can't help you. Please come again.

1. *large TV*

2. *comfortable rocking chair*

3. *good CD player*

4. *cheap watch*

5. *fast printer*

6. *elegant evening gown*

7. *small cell phone*

8. *lightweight video camera*

9. *powerful computer*

10. *tall bookcase*

11. *short novel*

12.

BOB'S BARGAIN DEPARTMENT STORE

Bob's Bargain Department Store is the cheapest store in town. However, even though it's the cheapest, it isn't the most popular. People don't shop there very often because the products are bad.* In fact, some people say the products there are the worst in town.

The furniture isn't very comfortable, the clothes aren't very fashionable, the appliances aren't very dependable, and the home entertainment products aren't very good. Besides that, the location isn't very convenient, and the salespeople aren't very helpful.

That's why people don't shop at Bob's Bargain Department Store very often, even though it's the cheapest store in town.

THE LORD AND LADY DEPARTMENT STORE

The Lord and Lady Department Store sells very good products. In fact, some people say the products there are the best in town.

They sell the most comfortable furniture, the most fashionable clothes, the most dependable appliances, and the best home entertainment products. And besides that, their location is the most convenient, and their salespeople are the most helpful in town.

However, even though the Lord and Lady Department Store is the best store in town, people don't shop there very often because it's also the most expensive.

* bad – worse – worst

THE SUPER SAVER DEPARTMENT STORE

The Super Saver Department Store is the most popular store in town. It isn't the cheapest, and it isn't the most expensive. It doesn't have the best products, and it doesn't have the worst.

The furniture isn't the most comfortable you can buy, but it's more comfortable than the furniture at many other stores. The clothes aren't the most fashionable you can buy, but they're more fashionable than the clothes at many other stores. The appliances aren't the most dependable you can buy, but they're more dependable than the appliances at many other stores. The home entertainment products aren't the best you can buy, but they're better than the home entertainment products at many other stores. In addition, the location is convenient, and the salespeople are helpful.

You can see why the Super Saver Department Store is the most popular store in town. The prices are reasonable, and the products are good. That's why people like to shop there.

READING *CHECK-UP*

TRUE OR FALSE?

1. Bob's Bargain Department Store is the most popular store in town.
2. The salespeople at Lord and Lady are more helpful than the salespeople at Super Saver.
3. The location of Lord and Lady isn't as convenient as the location of Bob's.
4. The Super Saver Department Store has the best prices in town.
5. The home entertainment products at Super Saver are better than the home entertainment products at Bob's.
6. People in this town say the cheapest department store is the best.

How About You?

Tell about places to shop where you live: the cheapest, the most expensive, the most popular. Tell about the products they sell.

INTERACTIONS *Sharing Opinions*

Practice conversations with other students. Share opinions, and give reasons for your opinions.

In your opinion, . . .

1. Who is the most popular actor/actress in your country? Who is the most popular TV star? the best singer?

2. What is the most popular car in your country? the most popular sport? the best newspaper? the most popular magazine? the best TV program? the most popular food?

3. What is the best city in your country? What is the worst city? Why? What are the most interesting tourist sights in your country? What are the most popular vacation places?

4. Who is the most important person in your country now? Why? Who was the most important person in the history of your country? Why?

Who is the most important person in your life? Why? Write about this person in your journal.

CHAPTER SUMMARY

GRAMMAR

SUPERLATIVES

He's	the smartest the nicest the biggest the busiest	person I know.
	the most talented the most interesting	

KEY VOCABULARY

DESCRIBING

bad–worse–worst	elegant	good–better–best	lazy	patient	sloppy
boring	energetic	helpful	lightweight	polite	small
bright	fashionable	honest	long	popular	smart
cheap	fast	horrible	mean	powerful	stubborn
comfortable	friendly	interesting	nice	pretty	talented
convenient	funny	kind	noisy	rude	ugly
dependable	generous	large	obnoxious	short	wonderful

Volume 2   Number 2

Did You Know?

The longest car in the world is 100 feet long. It has 26 wheels, a swimming pool, and a waterbed!

The world's biggest costume party is the Carnival celebration in Brazil. Every day during Carnival, more than 50,000 people walk through the streets in costumes.

The largest subway station in the world is Grand Central Terminal in New York City. Every day more than half a million people pass through the station.

The biggest igloo in the world is the Ice Hotel in Sweden. It has rooms for 150 guests. Every year workers have to rebuild the hotel because it melts in the spring!

FACT FILE

World Geography Facts

- The longest river in the world is the Nile. It is 4,180 miles (6,690 kilometers) long.

- The largest ocean in the world is the Pacific Ocean. It is 64,000,000 square miles (165,760,000 square kilometers).

- The highest mountain in the world is Mount Everest. It is 29,028 feet (8,848 meters) high.

- The biggest desert in the world is the Sahara. It is 3,500,270 square miles (9,065,000 square kilometers).

BUILD YOUR VOCABULARY!

Adjectives with Negative Prefixes

They're _____ .

■ uncomfortable

■ unfriendly

■ unhealthy

■ unsafe

■ impatient

■ impolite

■ inexpensive

■ dishonest

Recreation and Entertainment

The most popular type of outdoor recreation in France is camping. Every night 3 million people in France sleep outside.

Movies are the most popular type of entertainment in India. Every day 15 million people in India go to the movies.

The most popular sport in the world is football. This game is called "soccer" in the United States. More than 100,000,000 people play football in over 150 countries.

What are the most popular types of recreation and entertainment in different countries you know?

Global Exchange

IvanaG: I'm going on vacation with my family tomorrow. We're going to the most popular beach in our country. We'll stay there for a week in a small hotel. It isn't the best hotel there, but it's the friendliest and the closest to the beach. We go there every year. It's a lot of fun! The water is clear, and the air is fresh. My sister and my brother and I swim all day, and we go to an amusement park in the evening. I think it has the largest roller-coaster in the world! So I'll write again when I get back and tell you all about our vacation.

P.S. Do you have a favorite vacation place? Where is it? When do you go there? What do you do?

Send a message to a keypal. Tell about a favorite vacation place in your country.

LISTENING

And Now a Word From Our Sponsors!

_b_ **1** Rings & Things   **a.** furniture

____ **2** Big Value Store   **b.** jewelry

____ **3** Comfort Kingdom   **c.** sports equipment

____ **4** Electric City   **d.** appliances

____ **5** Recreation Station   **e.** home entertainment products

What Are They Saying?

The biggest!
The smallest!
The fastest!
The most exciting!

Imperatives
Directions

- **Getting Around Town**
- **Public Transportation**

VOCABULARY PREVIEW

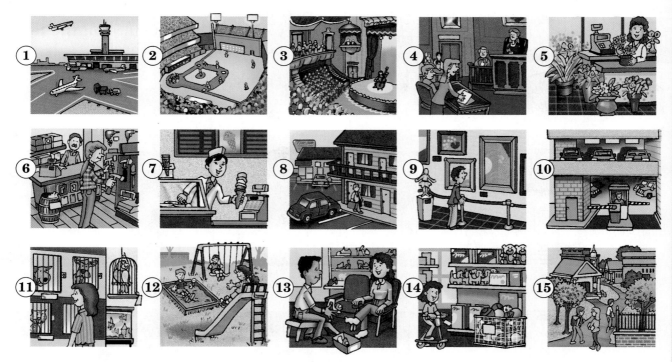

1. airport	6. hardware store	11. pet shop
2. baseball stadium	7. ice cream shop	12. playground
3. concert hall	8. motel	13. shoe store
4. courthouse	9. museum	14. toy store
5. flower shop	10. parking garage	15. university

Can You Tell Me How to Get to . . . ?

walk up walk down	on the right on the left	across from next to between

MAIN ST.

drug store | laundromat
barber shop | bakery
toy store | clinic
bank | shoe store
police station | high school
library | post office

POST OFFICE

laundromat?

A. Excuse me. Can you tell me how to get to the laundromat from here?

B. Sure. **Walk up** Main Street and you'll see the laundromat **on the right, across from** the drug store.

A. Thank you.

DRUG STORE

post office?

A. Excuse me. Can you tell me how to get to the post office from here?

B. Sure. **Walk down** Main Street and you'll see the post office **on the left, next to** the high school.

A. Thank you.

LIBRARY

1. *clinic?*

BAKERY

2. *police station?*

BANK

3. *drug store?*

LAUNDROMAT

4. *library?*

HIGH SCHOOL

5. *barber shop?*

POLICE STATION

6. *toy store?*

Could You Please Tell Me How to Get to . . . ?

walk along

on the right
on the left

across from
next to
between

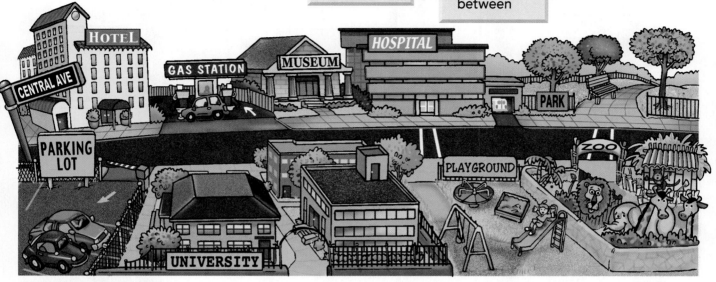

hospital?

A. Excuse me. Could you please tell me how to get to the hospital from here?

B. Sure. **Walk along** Central Avenue and you'll see the hospital **on the left, between** the museum and the park.

A. Thanks.

1. *museum?*

2. *university?*

3. *park?*

4. *hotel?*

5. *parking lot?*

6. *zoo?*

Would You Please Tell Me How to Get to . . . ?

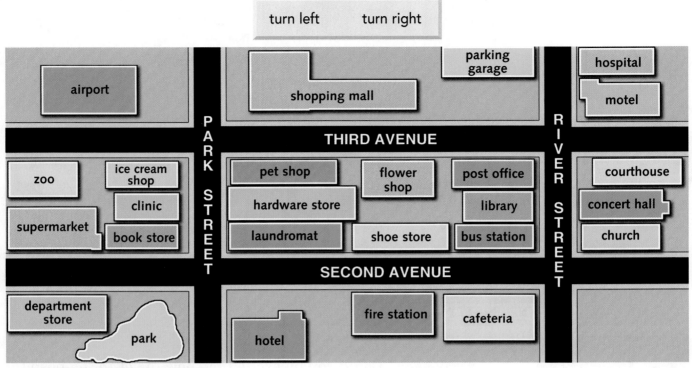

turn left   turn right

PARK STREET   **RIVER STREET**

THIRD AVENUE

SECOND AVENUE

airport   shopping mall   parking garage   hospital   motel

zoo   ice cream shop   pet shop   flower shop   post office   courthouse

clinic   hardware store   library   concert hall

supermarket   book store   laundromat   shoe store   bus station   church

department store   park   hotel   fire station   cafeteria

bus station?

A. Excuse me. Would you please tell me how to get to the bus station from here?

B. Certainly. **Walk up** Park Street to Second Avenue and **turn right**. **Walk along** Second Avenue and you'll see the bus station **on the left, across from** the cafeteria.

A. Thanks very much.

concert hall?

A. Excuse me. Would you please tell me how to get to the concert hall from here?

B. Certainly. **Drive along** Second Avenue to River Street and **turn left**. **Drive up** River Street and you'll see the concert hall **on the right, between** the courthouse and the church.

A. Thanks very much.

1. *hospital?*

2. *zoo?*

3. *shoe store?*

4. *laundromat?*

5. *supermarket?*

6. *post office?*

7. *clinic?*

8. *airport?*

9.

How to Say It!

Asking for Repetition

A. I'm sorry. Could you please { repeat that?
say that again? }

B. Sure. *Walk along . . .*

**Practice some conversations on this page again.
Ask people to repeat the directions.**

Take the Main Street Bus

A. Excuse me. What's the quickest way to get to Peter's Pet Shop?

B. **Take** the Main Street bus and **get off** at First Avenue. **Walk up** First Avenue and you'll see Peter's Pet Shop **on the right**.

A. Thank you very much.

B. You're welcome.

A. Excuse me. What's the easiest way to get to Harry's Barber Shop?

B. **Take** the subway and **get off** at Fourth Avenue. **Walk down** Fourth Avenue and you'll see Harry's Barber Shop **on the left**.

A. Thank you very much.

B. You're welcome.

1. What's the fastest way to get to the baseball stadium?

2. What's the best way to get to the library?

3. What's the most direct way to get to the zoo?

4. I'm in a hurry! What's the shortest way to get to the train station?

ROLE PLAY *Can You Tell Me How to Get There?*

A. Can you recommend **a good hotel**?

B. Yes. The Bellview is **a good hotel**. I think it's **one of the best hotels** in town.

A. Can you tell me how to get there?

B. Sure. Take the subway and get off at Brighton Boulevard. You'll see the Bellview at the corner of Brighton Boulevard and Twelfth Street.

A. Thank you very much.

B. You're welcome.

These people are visiting your city. Recommend real places you know and like, and give directions.

Can you recommend a good restaurant?

Can you recommend a big department store?

Can you recommend an interesting tourist sight?

Can you recommend _____?

HAROLD NEVER GOT THERE!

Dear Students,

Here are directions to my house. I'll see you at the party.

Your English teacher

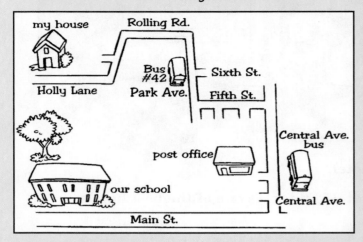

1. From our school, walk along Main St. to Central Ave. and turn left.

2. Walk up Central Ave. 2 blocks, and you'll see a bus stop at the corner, across from the post office.

3. Take the Central Ave. bus and get off at Fifth St.

4. Turn left and walk along Fifth St. 3 blocks to Park Ave. and turn right.

5. Walk up Park Ave. 1 block, and you'll see a bus stop at the corner of Park Ave. and Sixth St.

6. Take Bus #42 and get off at Rolling Rd.

7. Turn left and walk along Rolling Rd. 1 block.

8. Turn left again, and walk 2 blocks to Holly Lane and turn right.

9. Walk along Holly Lane. My house is the last one on the right.

Harold was very disappointed last night. All the other students in his English class went to a party at their teacher's house, but Harold never got there. He followed his teacher's directions, but he made one little mistake.

From their school, he walked along Main Street to Central Avenue and turned left. He walked up Central Avenue two blocks to the bus stop at the corner, across from the post office. He took the Central Avenue bus and got off at Fifth Street. He turned left and walked along Fifth Street three blocks to Park Avenue and turned right. He walked up Park Avenue one block to the bus stop at the corner of Park Avenue and Sixth Street.

He took Bus Number 42, but he got off at the wrong stop. He got off at River Road instead of Rolling Road. He turned left and walked along River Road one block. He turned left again and walked two blocks, turned right, and got completely lost.

Harold was very upset. He really wanted to go to the party last night, and he can't believe he made such a stupid mistake!

✔ READING CHECK-UP

TRUE OR FALSE?

1. Harold's English teacher lives on Holly Lane.
2. The Central Avenue bus stops across from the post office.
3. The teacher made one little mistake in the directions.
4. The school is on Main Street.
5. Harold took the wrong bus.
6. Bus Number 42 goes to Rolling Road.
7. Harold got off the bus at Rolling Road.
8. Harold didn't really want to go to the party last night.

WHAT'S THE WORD?

It's very easy to get _____1 the zoo from here. Walk up this street _____2 the corner and turn right. Walk two blocks and you'll see a bus stop _____3 the corner _____4 Grove Street and Fourth Avenue. Take the West Side bus and get _____5 _____6 Park Road. You'll see the zoo _____7 the left. It's next _____8 the library and across _____9 the museum.

LISTENING

WHAT'S THE WORD?

Listen and choose the word you hear.

1. a. right   b. left
2. a. right   b. left
3. a. down   b. up
4. a. along   b. down
5. a. to   b. on
6. a. off   b. of
7. a. on   b. at

WHERE ARE THEY?

Where are these people? Listen and choose the correct place.

1. a. department store   b. laundromat
2. a. pet shop   b. cafeteria
3. a. restaurant   b. library
4. a. hospital   b. hotel
5. a. barber shop   b. supermarket
6. a. parking lot   b. parking garage

IN YOUR OWN WORDS

FOR WRITING AND DISCUSSION

You're going to invite people to your home. Draw a map and write directions to help them get there. (Give them directions from your school.)

PRONUNCIATION *Could you & Would you*

Listen. Then say it.

Could you please tell me how to get
to the bank?

Could you please repeat that?

Would you please tell me how to get
to the library?

Say it. Then listen.

Could you please tell me how to
get to the park?

Could you please say that again?

Would you please tell me how to
get to the zoo?

How do you get to different places in your
community? Do you walk? Do you drive?
Do you take a bus, train, or subway? Is it
easy or difficult to get to these places?
Write about it in your journal.

CHAPTER SUMMARY

GRAMMAR

IMPERATIVES

Walk up Main Street.
Turn right.
Drive along Second Avenue to River Street.

KEY VOCABULARY

PLACES AROUND TOWN

airport	cafeteria	fire station	ice cream shop	parking lot	shopping mall
bakery	church	flower shop	laundromat	pet shop	supermarket
bank	clinic	gas station	library	playground	toy store
barber shop	concert hall	hardware store	motel	police station	train station
baseball stadium	courthouse	high school	museum	post office	university
book store	department store	hospital	park	restaurant	zoo
bus station	drug store	hotel	parking garage	shoe store	

Listening Scripts

Chapter 1 – Page 9

Listen and choose the correct answer.

1. What are you going to do tomorrow?
2. What do you do in the summer?
3. When did you clean your apartment?
4. What did you give your parents for their anniversary?
5. Where did you and your friends go yesterday?
6. How often do they send messages to each other?
7. What did he give her?
8. When are you going to make pancakes?

Chapter 2 – Page 16

Listen and choose what the people are talking about.

1. A. How much do you want?
   B. Just a little, please.
2. A. Do you want some more?
   B. Okay. But just a few.
3. A. These are delicious!
   B. I'm glad you like them.
4. A. I ate too many.
   B. How many did you eat?
5. A. They're bad for my health.
   B. Really?
6. A. It's very good.
   B. Thank you.
7. A. Would you care for some more?
   B. Yes, but not too much.
8. A. There isn't any.
   B. There isn't?!

Chapter 3 – Page 22

Listen and choose what the people are talking about.

1. A. How much does a gallon cost?
   B. Two seventy-nine.
2. A. They're very expensive this week.
   B. You're right.
3. A. How many loaves do we need?
   B. Three.
4. A. Sorry. There aren't any more.
   B. There aren't?!
5. A. I need two pounds.
   B. Two pounds? Okay.
6. A. How much does the large box cost?
   B. Five thirty-nine.
7. A. How many cans do we need?
   B. Three.
8. A. I bought too much.
   B. Really?

Side by Side Gazette – Page 28

Listen and match the products and the prices.

1. Attention, food shoppers! Thank you for shopping at Save-Rite Supermarket! Crispy Cereal is on sale this week. A box of Crispy Cereal is only three dollars and forty-nine cents. Three forty-nine is a very good price for Crispy Cereal. So buy some today!
2. Attention, shoppers! Right now in the bakery section whole wheat bread is on sale. Buy a loaf of whole wheat bread for only two seventy-five. That's right! Just two seventy-five! The bread is hot and fresh. So come to the bakery section and get a loaf now!
3. Thank you for shopping at Sunny Supermarket! We have a special low price on orange juice today. A quart of orange juice is only a dollar seventy-nine. Orange juice is in Aisle 5, next to the milk.
4. Hello, food shoppers! It's 95 degrees today. It's a good day for Sorelli's ice cream! Sorelli's ice cream comes in vanilla, chocolate, and other delicious flavors. And today, a pint of Sorelli's ice cream is only three twenty-five!
5. Welcome to Bartley's Supermarket! We have a special today on bananas. You can buy bananas for only forty cents a pound. Bananas are good for you! So walk over to our fruit section and buy a bunch of bananas today!

Chapter 4 – Page 37

WHAT'S THE LINE?

Mrs. Harris (from the story on page 36) is calling Tommy and Julie's school. Listen and choose the correct lines.

1. Good morning. Park Elementary School.
2. Yes, Mrs. Harris. What can I do for you?
3. Oh? What's the matter?
4. That's too bad. Are you going to take them to the doctor?
5. Well, I hope Tommy and Julie feel better soon.

WHAT'S THE WORD?

Listen and choose the word you hear.

1. I might go to school tomorrow.
2. I want to come to work today.
3. Don't walk there!
4. We'll be ready in half an hour.
5. They'll go to school tomorrow.
6. Don't stand there! You might get hit!
7. I call the doctor when I'm sick.
8. Watch your step! There are wet spots on the floor.
9. I'm sick and tired of sailing.

Chapter 5 – Page 44

Listen and choose what the people are talking about.

1. A. I like it. It's fast.
   B. It is. It's much faster than my old one.
2. A. Is it comfortable?
   B. Yes. It's more comfortable than my old one.
3. A. I think it should be shorter.
   B. But it's very short now!
4. A. They aren't very polite.
   B. You're right. They should be more polite.
5. A. Is it safe?
   B. Yes. It's much safer than my old one.
6. A. Which one should I buy?
   B. Buy this one. It's more powerful than that one.

Chapter 6 – Page 53

Listen to the sentence. Is the person saying something good or something bad about someone else?

1. She's the nicest person I know.
2. He's the laziest student in our class.
3. He's the most boring person I know.
4. She's the most generous person in our family.
5. They're the most honest people I know.
6. He's the rudest person in our apartment building.
7. He's the most dependable person in our office.
8. She's the kindest neighbor on our street.
9. She's the most stubborn person I know.

Side by Side Gazette – Page 60

Listen and match the products.

ANNOUNCER: Are you looking for a special gift for a special person in your life? A birthday gift? An anniversary present? Come to Rings & Things—the best store in town for rings, necklaces, earrings, bracelets, and other fine things. Rings & Things—on Main Street downtown, or at the East Side Mall.

FRIEND 1: That was an excellent dinner!
FRIEND 2: Thank you. I'm glad you liked it.
FRIEND 1: Can I help you wash the dishes?
FRIEND 2: Thanks. But they're already in the dishwasher.
FRIEND 1: Is your dishwasher on?
FRIEND 2: Yes, it is.
FRIEND 1: I can't believe it! Your dishwasher is MUCH quieter than mine.
FRIEND 2: It's new. We got it at the Big Value Store. They sell the quietest dishwashers in town.
ANNOUNCER: That's right. The Big Value Store sells the quietest dishwashers in town. We also have the largest refrigerators, the most powerful washing machines, and the best ovens. And we also have the best prices! So come to the Big Value Store, on Airport Road, open seven days a week.

PERSON WHO CAN'T FALL ASLEEP: Oh, I can't believe it! It's three o'clock in the morning, and I can't fall asleep. This bed is so uncomfortable! I need a new bed. I need a new bed NOW!
ANNOUNCER: Do you have this problem? Is your bed uncomfortable? Come to Comfort Kingdom for the most comfortable beds you can buy. We also have the most beautiful sofas and the most attractive tables and chairs in the city. And our salespeople are the friendliest and the most helpful in town. So visit Comfort Kingdom today because life is short, and you should be comfortable!

ANNOUNCER: I'm standing here today in front of Electric City so we can talk to a typical customer. Here's a typical customer now. He's leaving the store with a large box. Let's ask him a question. Excuse me, sir. May I ask you a question?
CUSTOMER: Certainly.
ANNOUNCER: What did you buy today?
CUSTOMER: A VCR.
ANNOUNCER: And why did you buy it at Electric City?
CUSTOMER: Because Electric City has the cheapest and the most dependable products in town.
ANNOUNCER: Is this your first time at Electric City?
CUSTOMER: Oh, no! Last year I bought a radio here, and the year before I bought a TV.
ANNOUNCER: And are you happy with those products?
CUSTOMER: Absolutely! The radio is much better than my old one, and the picture on my TV is much bigger and brighter.
ANNOUNCER: So are you a happy customer?
CUSTOMER: Definitely! There's no place like Electric City. It's the best store in town.
ANNOUNCER: Well, there you have it! Another happy Electric City customer. Visit an Electric City store near YOU today!

ANNOUNCER: This is it! It's the biggest sale of the year, and it's this weekend at Recreation Station! That's right. Everything is on sale—sneakers, tennis rackets, footballs, basketballs—everything in the store! It's all on sale at Recreation Station. We're the largest! We're the most convenient! We're the best! And this weekend we're the cheapest! It's the biggest sale of the year, and it's this weekend—only at Recreation Station!

WHAT'S THE WORD?

Listen and choose the word you hear.

1. The clinic is on the right, next to the post office.
2. The library is on the left, across from the park.
3. Walk up Town Road to Main Street.
4. Drive along Fourth Avenue to Station Street.
5. Take the subway to Pond Road.
6. The bus stop is at the corner of Central Avenue and Fifth.
7. Take this bus and get off at Bond Street.

WHERE ARE THEY?

Where are these people? Listen and choose the correct place.

1. **A.** Do you want to buy this shirt?
   B. Yes, please.

2. **A.** Please give me an order of chicken.
   B. An order of chicken? Certainly.

3. **A.** Shh! Please be quiet! People are reading.
   B. Sorry.

4. **A.** Can I visit my wife?
   B. Yes. She and the baby are in Room 407.

5. **A.** How much does one head cost?
   B. A dollar fifty-nine.

6. **A.** Hmm. Where's our car?
   B. I think it's on the third floor.

Cardinal Numbers

1	one	20	twenty
2	two	21	twenty-one
3	three	22	twenty-two
4	four	.	.
5	five	.	.
6	six	29	twenty-nine
7	seven	30	thirty
8	eight	40	forty
9	nine	50	fifty
10	ten	60	sixty
11	eleven	70	seventy
12	twelve	80	eighty
13	thirteen	90	ninety
14	fourteen		
15	fifteen	100	one hundred
16	sixteen	200	two hundred
17	seventeen	300	three hundred
18	eighteen	.	.
19	nineteen	.	.
		900	nine hundred
		1,000	one thousand
		2,000	two thousand
		3,000	three thousand
		.	.
		10,000	ten thousand
		100,000	one hundred thousand
		1,000,000	one million

Ordinal Numbers

1st	first	20th	twentieth
2nd	second	21st	twenty-first
3rd	third	22nd	twenty-second
4th	fourth	.	.
5th	fifth	.	.
6th	sixth	29th	twenty-ninth
7th	seventh	30th	thirtieth
8th	eighth	40th	fortieth
9th	ninth	50th	fiftieth
10th	tenth	60th	sixtieth
11th	eleventh	70th	seventieth
12th	twelfth	80th	eightieth
13th	thirteenth	90th	ninetieth
14th	fourteenth		
15th	fifteenth	100th	one hundredth
16th	sixteenth	1,000th	one thousandth
17th	seventeenth	1,000,000th	one millionth
18th	eighteenth		
19th	nineteenth		

How to Read a Date

June 9, 1941 = "June ninth, nineteen forty-one"

November 16, 2010 = "November sixteenth, two thousand ten" *or*

"November sixteenth, two thousand and ten"

Irregular Verbs: Past Tense

be	was	lead	led
become	became	leave	left
begin	began	lend	lent
bite	bit	lose	lost
build	built	make	made
break	broke	meet	met
buy	bought	put	put
catch	caught	read	read
come	came	ride	rode
cost	cost	run	ran
cut	cut	say	said
do	did	see	saw
drink	drank	sell	sold
drive	drove	send	sent
eat	ate	shake	shook
fall	fell	sing	sang
feed	fed	sit	sat
feel	felt	sleep	slept
find	found	speak	spoke
fly	flew	spend	spent
forget	forgot	stand	stood
get	got	steal	stole
give	gave	swim	swam
go	went	take	took
grow	grew	teach	taught
have	had	tell	told
hear	heard	think	thought
hurt	hurt	understand	understood
keep	kept	wear	wore
know	knew	write	wrote

Index

ACTIVITY WORKBOOK

SIDE by SIDE

THIRD EDITION

BOOK 2A

Steven J. Molinsky
Bill Bliss

with

Carolyn Graham • Peter S. Bliss

Contributing Authors

Dorothy Lynde • Elizabeth Handley

Illustrated by
Richard E. Hill

CONTENTS

A WHAT DO THEY LIKE TO DO?

chat online	go hiking	go to the mall	play soccer	write letters
go dancing	go to the beach	listen to music	watch TV	

1. He _____ likes to _____

    _____ watch TV _____ .

2. They _____

    _____ .

3. She _____

    _____ .

4. I _____

    _____ .

5. They _____

    _____ .

6. He _____

    _____ .

7. She _____

    _____ .

8. We _____

    _____ .

9. My dog _____

    _____ .

B LISTENING

Listen and choose the correct response.

1. a. He likes to chat online.
    b. They like to chat online.

2. a. I like to dance.
    b. She likes to dance.

3. a. He likes to read.
    b. She likes to read.

4. a. They like to play basketball.
    b. We like to play basketball.

5. a. He likes to go to the library.
    b. We like to go to the library.

6. a. You like to go to the mall.
    b. I like to go to the mall.

7. a. We like to play loud music.
    b. He likes to play loud music.

8. a. She likes to watch TV.
    b. They like to watch TV.

WHAT DO THEY LIKE TO DO?

bake	go	listen	ride	sing	watch

1. Alan likes to _____watch_____ TV.

_____He watches_____ TV every day.

_____He watched_____ TV yesterday.

_____He's going to watch_____ TV tomorrow.

2. I like to _____ to music.

_____ to music every day.

_____ to music yesterday.

_____ to music tomorrow.

3. Thelma likes to _____ her bicycle.

_____ her bicycle every day.

_____ her bicycle yesterday.

_____ her bicycle tomorrow.

4. My parents like to _____.

_____ every day.

_____ yesterday.

_____ tomorrow.

5. My wife and I like to _____ cookies.

_____ cookies every day.

_____ cookies yesterday.

_____ cookies tomorrow.

6. Brian likes to _____ sailing.

_____ sailing every day.

_____ sailing yesterday.

_____ sailing tomorrow.

D LIKES AND DISLIKES

| clean | cook | drive | eat | feed | go | read | take | wait | watch |

like to
likes to

don't like to
doesn't like to

1. Ronald ___likes to cook___ spaghetti.

2. Sally ___doesn't like to take___ the subway.

3. My children _____ the birds in the park.

4. Ted and Amy _____ in noisy restaurants.

5. My wife _____ novels.

6. Arnold _____ for the bus.

7. My friends and I _____ videos.

8. I _____ downtown.

9. Howard _____ his house.

10. Tim and Jim _____ to the doctor.

WRITE ABOUT YOURSELF

What do you like to do?

I like to ....

I ....

I ....

I ....

I ....

What don't you like to do?

I don't like to ....

I ....

I ....

I ....

I ....

F **DAY AFTER DAY**

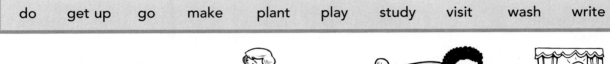

| do | get up | go | make | plant | play | study | visit | wash | write |

1. Tim _____*washes*_____ his car every day.

   _____*He washed*_____ his car yesterday.

   _____*He's going to wash*_____ his car tomorrow.

3. Millie and Max _____ dancing every Friday.

   _____ dancing last Friday.

   _____ dancing next Friday.

2. Alice _____ early every morning.

   _____ early yesterday morning.

   _____ early tomorrow morning.

4. I _____ English every evening.

   _____ English yesterday evening.

   _____ English tomorrow evening.

(continued)

5. The man next door _____ the drums every night.

_____ the drums last night.

_____ the drums tomorrow night.

6. My mother _____ pancakes for breakfast every Sunday.

_____ pancakes last Sunday.

_____ pancakes next Sunday.

7. My wife and I _____ flowers every spring.

_____ flowers last spring.

_____ flowers next spring.

8. Steven _____ to his girlfriend every week.

_____ to her last week.

_____ to her next week.

9. Julie _____ her grandparents every weekend.

_____ them last weekend.

_____ them next weekend.

10. My husband and I _____ yoga every afternoon.

_____ yoga yesterday afternoon.

_____ yoga tomorrow afternoon.

11. I _____ every _____ .

_____

_____

G GrammarRap: *I Don't Like to Rush*

Listen. Then clap and practice.

I   don't like to   rush.   Do you?

I   don't like to   hurry.

I   don't like to   get   upset.

I   don't like to   worry.

I'm not   going to   rush.   Are you?

I'm not   going to   hurry.

I'm not   going to   get   upset.

I'm not   going to   worry!

H GrammarRap: *He Doesn't Like to Watch TV*

Listen. Then clap and practice.

He doesn't   like to   watch   TV.

He doesn't   like to   dance.

He doesn't   like to   cook or   sew

or wash or   iron his   pants.

She doesn't   like to   go to the   beach.

She doesn't   like to   shop.

She doesn't   like to   vacuum her   rugs

or dust or   wax or   mop.

Activity Workbook   **7**

I WHAT'S PAULA GOING TO GIVE HER FAMILY?

Paula is looking for presents for her family.
Here's what she's going to give them.

1. Her husband's hands are always cold.   _She's going to give him gloves._

2. Her daughter loves animals.   _____

3. Her son never arrives on time.   _____

4. Her parents like to listen to music.   _____

5. Her sister likes clothes.   _____

6. Her brother likes to read.   _____

7. Her grandparents like flowers.   _____

8. Her cousin Charlie likes to talk to his friends.   _____

J PRESENTS

1. Last year I ___gave___ my husband
   pajamas.

   This year ___I'm going to give him___
   a bathrobe.

2. Last year Bobby _____ his grandmother
   candy.

   This year _____
   flowers.

3. Last year Carol _____ her boyfriend
   a tee shirt.

   This year _____
   sweat pants.

4. Last year we _____ our children
   a bird.

   This year _____
   a dog.

5. Last year I _____ my girlfriend
   perfume.

   This year _____
   a ring.

6. Last year we _____ our son
   a sweater.

   This year _____
   a bicycle.

7. Last year I ....

   This year ....

   ....

he	her	him	I	me	she	they	them	us	we	you

1. A. What did you give your wife for her birthday?

   B. _____I_____ gave _____her_____ earrings.

2. A. What did your children give you for your birthday?

   B. _____ gave _____ a book.

3. A. What did Michael give his parents for their anniversary?

   B. _____ gave _____ a CD player.

4. A. What did your friends give you and your husband for your anniversary?

   B. _____ gave _____ a plant.

5. A. What did your wife give you for your birthday?

   B. _____ gave _____ a briefcase.

6. A. What did you and your wife give your son for his birthday?

   B. _____ gave _____ a bicycle.

7. A. I forget. What did you give me for my last birthday?

   B. _____ gave _____ a painting.

8. A. I forget. What did I give you for *your* last birthday?

   B. _____ gave _____ a dress.

1st	first	7th	seventh	13th	thirteenth	19th	nineteenth	50th	fiftieth
2nd	second	8th	eighth	14th	fourteenth	20th	twentieth	60th	sixtieth
3rd	third	9th	ninth	15th	fifteenth	21st	twenty-first	70th	seventieth
4th	fourth	10th	tenth	16th	sixteenth	22nd	twenty-second	80th	eightieth
5th	fifth	11th	eleventh	17th	seventeenth	30th	thirtieth	90th	ninetieth
6th	sixth	12th	twelfth	18th	eighteenth	40th	fortieth	100th	one hundredth

L MATCHING

_b_ 1. eighth   **a.** 2nd

____ 2. one hundredth   **b.** 8th

____ 3. second   **c.** 20th

____ 4. twentieth   **d.** 100th

____ 5. thirty-third   **e.** 14th

____ 6. thirteenth   **f.** 13th

____ 7. fourteenth   **g.** 40th

____ 8. fortieth   **h.** 33rd

M WHAT'S THE NUMBER?

1. fiftieth   _50th_

2. ninety-ninth   _____

3. fifteenth   _____

4. twelfth   _____

5. seventy-seventh   _____

6. first   _____

7. sixteenth   _____

8. sixty-fifth   _____

9. eighty-fourth   _____

10. thirty-sixth   _____

N LISTENING

Listen and write the ordinal number you hear.

1. barber shop   _2nd_

2. Wong family   _____

3. Acme Company   _____

4. Bob Richards   _____

5. bank   _____

6. dentist's office   _____

7. flower shop   _____

8. Martinez family   _____

9. Louise Lane   _____

10. computer store   _____

11. French restaurant _____

12. my apartment   _____

13. Park family   _____

14. Dr. Jacobson   _____

15. Walker family   _____

16. health club   _____

O RICHARD'S BIRTHDAYS

Fill in the missing words.

On Richard's 7th birthday, he (have) ___had___¹ a party at home. His mother (make) _____² pizza, and his father (bake) _____³ a cake. Richard's parents (give) _____⁴ him a new dog. Richard's friends (love) _____⁵ his birthday party because they (play) _____⁶ with his new dog, but Richard was upset because his mother didn't (give) _____⁷ the dog any cake to eat.

On Richard's 10th birthday, he (go) _____⁸ to the beach with his friends. They (swim) _____⁹ at the beach, and they (go) _____¹⁰ to a restaurant to eat. Richard's friends (like) _____¹¹ his birthday party, but Richard was upset because he didn't (like) _____¹² his present. His friends (give) _____¹³ him a wallet, but he (want) _____¹⁴ a baseball.

On Richard's 13th birthday, he (have) _____¹⁵ a picnic. His mother (cook) _____¹⁶ hot dogs and hamburgers. They (eat)_____¹⁷ delicious food and (play) _____¹⁸ baseball. All of his friends (enjoy) _____¹⁹ his birthday party, but Richard was upset because the girls didn't (talk) _____²⁰ to him.

On Richard's 16th birthday, he didn't (have) _____²¹ a party. He (go) _____²² dancing with his girlfriend, and he (have) _____²³ a wonderful time. His friends didn't (give) _____²⁴ him presents and his parents didn't (cook) _____²⁵. But Richard wasn't upset because he (dance) _____²⁶ with his girlfriend all night.

P MATCHING

_b_	1.	Richard didn't like his present _____.	a.	on his 7th birthday
____	2.	He went dancing _____.	b.	on his 10th birthday
____	3.	His parents gave him a dog _____.	c.	on his 13th birthday
____	4.	The girls didn't talk to Richard _____.	d.	on his 16th birthday

apples	cheese	ice cream	meat	pepper
bread	eggs	ketchup	mustard	potatoes
cake	flour	lettuce	onions	soy sauce
carrots	grapes	mayonnaise	oranges	tomatoes

1. ___tomatoes___ 2. _____ 3. _____ 4. _____

5. _____ 6. _____ 7. _____ 8. _____

9. _____ 10. _____ 11. _____ 12. _____

13. _____ 14. _____ 15. _____ 16. _____

17. _____ 18. _____ 19. _____ 20. _____

B WHAT ARE THEY SAYING?

Where's	Where are	It's	They're

1. A. _____Where's_____ the butter?

   B. _____It's_____ in the refrigerator.

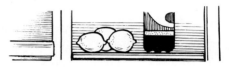

2. A. _____Where are_____ the bananas?

   B. _____They're_____ on the counter.

3. A. _____ the salt?

   B. _____ in the cabinet.

4. A. _____ the lemons?

   B. _____ in the refrigerator.

5. A. _____ the cookies?

   B. _____ in the cabinet.

6. A. _____ the chicken?

   B. _____ in the freezer.

7. A. _____ the pears?

   B. _____ on the counter.

8. A. _____ the rice?

   B. _____ in the cabinet.

C LISTENING

Listen and choose the correct response.

1. a. It's on the counter.
   b. They're on the counter.

2. a. It's in the refrigerator.
   b. They're in the refrigerator.

3. a. It's in the freezer.
   b. They're in the freezer.

4. a. It's in the cabinet.
   b. They're in the cabinet.

5. a. It's on the counter.
   b. They're on the counter.

6. a. It's in the cabinet.
   b. They're in the cabinet.

7. a. It's on the counter.
   b. They're on the counter.

8. a. It's in the refrigerator.
   b. They're in the refrigerator.

D I'M SORRY, BUT...

Look at the menu to see what Randy's Restaurant has and doesn't have today.

Today's Menu
spaghetti
hamburgers
salad
ice cream
apple pie
milk
soda

1. A. May I have a hamburger and some french fries?

    B. I'm sorry, but _____ there aren't _____

    _____ any french fries _____ .

2. A. May I please have a salad and some tea?

    B. I'm sorry, but _____ there isn't _____

    _____ any tea _____ .

3. A. May I have chicken and some milk?

    B. I'm sorry, but _____

    _____ .

4. A. May I have ice cream and some cookies?

    B. I'm sorry, but _____

    _____ .

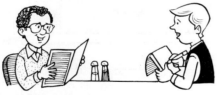

5. A. May I have cake and some soda?

    B. I'm sorry, but _____

    _____ .

6. A. May we have two sandwiches, please?

    B. I'm sorry, but _____

    _____ .

7. A. May I have apple pie and some orange juice?

    B. I'm sorry, but _____

    _____ .

8. A. May I have spaghetti and some meatballs?

    B. I'm sorry, but _____

    _____ .

E THERE ISN'T/THERE AREN'T

1. There ___isn't any mayonnaise___.

   How about some ___mustard___?

2. There ___aren't any bananas___.

   How about some ___grapes___?

3. There _____.

   How about some _____?

4. There _____.

   How about some _____?

5. There _____.

   How about some _____?

6. There _____.

   How about some _____?

7. There _____.

   How about some _____?

8. There _____.

   How about some _____?

F LISTENING

Listen and put a check (✓) under the correct picture.

1. _____   ✔   2. _____   _____   3. _____   _____

4. _____   _____   5. _____   _____   6. _____   _____

Activity Workbook   **15**

G WHAT'S THE WORD?

how much	too much	how many	too many	a little	a few

1. A. _____How many_____ meatballs do you want?

   B. Not _____too many_____.

   Just _____a few_____.

2. A. _____How much_____ cheese do you want?

   B. Not _____too much_____.

   Just _____a little_____.

3. A. _____ ice cream do you want?

   B. Not _____.

   Just _____.

4. A. _____ cookies do you want?

   B. Not _____.

   Just _____.

5. A. _____ lemonade do you want?

   B. Not _____.

   Just _____.

6. A. _____ oranges do you want?

   B. Not _____.

   Just _____.

H WHAT'S THE PROBLEM?

too much	too many

1. She cooked _____too many_____ meatballs.

2. He drinks _____ soda.

3. They ate _____ ice cream.

4. Henry had _____ onions.

16   Activity Workbook

1 GRAMMARRAP: *Just a Little, Just a Few*

Listen. Then clap and practice.

A.   How much   salt should I   put in the   soup?

B.   Just   a little,   not too   much.

A.   How many   onions should I   put in the   salad?

B.   Just   a few,   not too   many.

A.   How much   pepper should I   put in the   stew?

B.   Just   a little,   not too   much.

A.   How many   eggs should I   put in the   omelet?

B.   Just   a few,   not too   many.

A.   How much   sugar should I   put in the   tea?

B.   Just   a little,   not too   much.

All. Salt in the   soup,

      Pepper in the   stew,

      Eggs in the   omelet,

      Just   a few.

      Just   a little,   not too   much.

      Not too   many,   just   a few.

      Just   a few,   not too   many.

      Not too   many,   just one or   two.

little	much	this	is	it's	it
few	many	these	are	they're	them

1. A. Would you care for some more chocolate cake?

   B. Yes, please. But only a ___little___.

   My dentist says I eat too ___much___ chocolate cake.

2. A. Would you care for some more french fries?

   B. Yes, please. But only a _____.

   My wife says I eat too _____ french fries.

3. A. _____ pizza _____ fantastic.

   B. I'm glad you like _____. Would you care for a _____ more?

   A. Yes, please.

4. A. _____ potatoes _____ good.

   B. I'm glad you like _____. Would you care for a _____ more?

   A. No, thank you.

5. A. Would you like a _____ yogurt?

   B. Yes, please. My doctor says _____ good for my health.

6. A. Would you care for some cookies? I baked _____ this morning.

   B. Yes, please. But just a _____.

7. A. Would you care for some more pie?

   B. Yes, please. I know _____ bad for my health, but I really like _____.

8. A. You're eating too _____ meatballs!

   B. I know. But _____ really good. Can I have just a _____ more?

K MATCHING

__e__   1.   This pie is very good!   **a.** We can't. There isn't any flour.

_____   2.   How do you like the hamburgers?   **b.** I think it's delicious.

_____   3.   I think these cookies are excellent!   **c.** Just a little.

_____   4.   How much rice do you want?   **d.** They're on the counter.

_____   5.   Where's the tea?   **e.** I'm glad you like it.

_____   6.   Let's make some lemonade!   **f.** Just a few.

_____   7.   How do you like the pizza?   **g.** We can't. There aren't any lemons.

_____   8.   Where are the bananas?   **h.** I'm glad you like them.

_____   9.   How many carrots do you want?   **i.** It's in the cabinet.

_____   10.   Let's bake a cake for dessert!   **j.** I think they're delicious.

L LISTENING

Listen and put a check (✓) under the correct picture.

1. _____   ✓   2. _____   _____

3. _____   _____   4. _____   _____

5.  _____   _____   6. _____   _____

7. 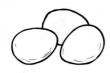 _____   _____   8.  _____   _____

9.  _____    _____   10. _____    _____

Listen. Then clap and practice.

All. Not too much, just a little,
Not too many, just a few.
Not too much, just a little,
Not too many, just a few.

A. Would you like more chicken?
B. Just a little.
A. Would you like more carrots?
B. Just a few.
A. Would you like more gravy?
B. Just a little.
A. Would you like more mushrooms?
B. Just a few.
A. Would you like more salad?
B. Just a little.
A. Would you like more tomatoes?
B. Just a few.
A. Would you like more coffee?
B. Just a little.
A. Would you like more cookies?
B. Just a few.

All. Not too much, just a little.
Not too many, just a few.
Not too much, just a little.
Not too many, just a few.

| bag | bunch | can | gallon | jar | loaf/loaves |
| bottle | box | dozen | head | pound | of |

1. Jack is going to buy food at the supermarket.

Jack's Shopping List

a _____can_____ ___of___ soup

a _____ _____ lettuce

a _____ _____ ketchup

a _____ _____ cheese

a _____ _____ flour

2. Jennifer is going to make breakfast for her parents.

Jennifer's Shopping List

a _____ _____ cereal

a _____ _____ jam

a _____ _____ bread

a _____ _____ bananas

a _____ _____ eggs

3. Mr. and Mrs. Baxter are going to have a birthday party for their daughter.

The Baxters' Shopping List

3 _____ _____ ice cream

2 _____ _____ cookies

2 _____ _____ grapes

3 _____ _____ meat

2 _____ _____ bread

4. What are YOU going to buy this week?

Your Shopping List

....

....

....

....

....

B WHAT ARE THEY SAYING?

| bananas | cheese | cookies | ice cream | jam | onions |

1. Do we need anything from the supermarket?

   Do we need anything else?

   Yes. We need a jar of ___jam___.

   Yes. We need a pint of _____.

2. What do we need from the supermarket?

   Do we need anything else?

   We need a bunch of _____.

   Yes. We need a box of _____.

3. Do we need anything from the supermarket?

   Do we need anything else?

   Yes. We need a bag of _____.

   Yes. We need a half a pound of _____.

C LISTENING

Listen to the conversations. Put a check (✓) under the foods you hear.

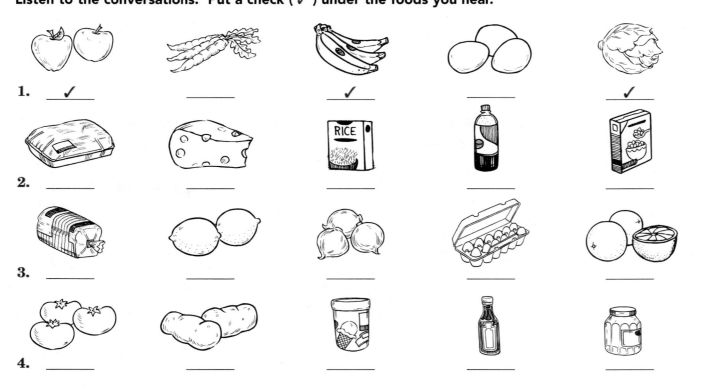

1. ___✓___   _____   ___✓___   _____   ___✓___

2. _____   _____   _____   _____   _____

3. _____   _____   _____   _____   _____

4. _____   _____   _____   _____   _____

22   Activity Workbook

GRAMMARRAP: *We Need Food*

Listen. Then clap and practice.

All.   We need   bread.

          Whole wheat bread.

A.   How many   loaves do we need?

All.   Two.

All.   We need   beans.

          Black   beans.

B.   How many   cans do we need?

All.   Three.

All.   We need   rice.

          Brown   rice.

C.   How many   pounds do we need?

All.   Four.

All.   We need   jam.

          Strawberry   jam.

D.   How many   jars do we   need?

All.   Five.

All.   We need   milk.

          Fresh   milk.

E.   How many   quarts do we need?

All.   Six.

All.   We need   cash.

          We need   money.

F.   How much   money do we need?

All.   A lot!

E SHOPPING FOR FOOD

| are | cost | does | loaf | money | of | quart |
| bread | costs | is | loaves | much | pound | right |

1. A. How __much__ does a _____ of milk _____?

   B. A _____ of _____ _____ two thirty-nine.

   A. Two dollars and thirty-nine cents?! That's a lot of _____!

   B. You're _____. Milk _____ very expensive this week.

2. A. How _____ does a _____ _____ bread cost?

   B. A _____ of _____ _____ one twenty-nine.

   A. Good! I'll take six _____, please.

   B. Six _____?! That's a lot _____ bread!

   A. I know. But _____ _____ very cheap this week!

3. A. How _____ _____ a _____ of apples cost?

   B. A _____ _____ apples _____ three sixty-five.

   A. Three sixty five?! That's too _____ money!

   B. You're right. Apples _____ very expensive today,

   but bananas _____ very cheap.

   A. That's nice. But how can I make an apple pie with bananas?!

F LISTENING

Listen and circle the price you hear.

1. $1.95   ($1.99)   4. $25   25¢   7. $3.13 $3.30

2. $5   5¢   5. $2.74 $2.47   8. $1.15 $1.50

3. $4.79 $9.47   6. $6.60 $6.16   9. $2.10 $21

G WHAT'S THE WORD?

1. A. What would you like for breakfast?
   B. Please give me an order of _____.
      a. cereal
      b. (b.) scrambled eggs

2. A. What would you like to drink?
   B. I want a glass of _____.
      a. milk
      b. coffee

3. A. What would you like for lunch?
   B. I want a bowl of _____.
      a. pancakes
      b. soup

4. A. Would you care for some dessert?
   B. Yes. I'd like a dish of _____.
      a. ice cream
      b. hot chocolate

5. A. What would you like?
   B. Please give me a cup of _____.
      a. tea
      b. cake

6. A. What would you like for dessert?
   B. I'd like a piece of _____.
      a. strawberries
      b. apple pie

H WHERE WOULD YOU LIKE TO GO FOR LUNCH?

are	glass	many	order
bowl	is	much	piece
cup	it	of	they
dish			

A. Where would you like to go for lunch?

B. Let's go to Carla's Cafe. Their spaghetti ___is___ 1 out of this world and _____ 2

   isn't expensive. I had an _____ 3 _____ 4 spaghetti there last week for
   a dollar ninety-five.

A. I don't really want to go to Carla's Cafe. Their spaghetti _____ 5 very good, but you can't get

   any chocolate milk. I like to have a _____ 6 of chocolate milk with my lunch.

B. How about The Pancake Place? Their pancakes _____ 7 fantastic, and _____ 8

   aren't expensive. An _____ 9 _____ 10 pancakes costs two sixty-nine.

A. I really don't like The Pancake Place. The pancakes _____ 11 tasty, but their salad

   _____ 12 terrible! It has too _____ 13 lettuce and too _____ 14 onions.

B. Well, how about Rita's Restaurant? Their desserts are wonderful. You can get a delicious

   _____ 15 _____ 16 pie, a _____ 17 _____ 18 strawberries, or a _____ 19 _____ 20
   ice cream.

A. I know. But their hot chocolate _____ 21 very bad. I like to have a _____ 22 _____ 23 hot
   chocolate with my dessert.

B. Wait a minute! I know where we can go for lunch. Let's go to YOUR house!

Listen. Then clap and practice.

We need a loaf of   bread

And a jar of   jam,

A box of   cookies

And a pound of   ham.

A bottle of   ketchup,

A pound of   cheese,

A dozen   eggs,

And a can of   peas.

A head of   lettuce,

Half a pound of   rice,

A bunch of   bananas,

And a bag of   ice.

a loaf of bread
a jar of jam
a box of cookies
a pound of ham
a bottle of ketchup

J **GRAMMARRAP:** *What Would You Like to Have?*

Listen. Then clap and practice.

A.   What would you like to   order?

     What would you like to   have?

B.   An order of   chicken,   a dish of   potatoes,

     A large green   salad   with a lot of   tomatoes.

     A bowl of   soup,   an order of   rice,

     And a glass of   soda   with a lot of   ice.

A.   And what would you like for   dessert?

B.   Nothing,   thanks.   I'm not very   hungry!

K WHAT'S THE WORD?

1. Slice the [honey / (carrots)] .

2. Cut up the [oranges / salt] .

3. Chop up the [flour / nuts] .

4. Pour in the [water / potatoes] .

5. Slice the [baking soda / apples] .

6. Pour it into the mixing [bowl / recipe] .

7. [Mix in / Put] the raisins.

8. [Add / Cook] for two hours.

L WHAT'S THE RECIPE?

[a little   a few]

Millie's Tomato Sauce

1. Put ___a little___ butter into a pan.

2. Chop up _____ onions.

3. Cut up _____ mushrooms and _____ cheese.

4. Slice _____ tomatoes.

5. Add _____ salt and _____ pepper.

6. Cook for _____ minutes.

M LISTENING

Listen and choose the correct word to complete the sentence.

1. a. onions
   b. water

2. a. cheese
   b. nuts

3. a. oranges
   b. baking soda

4. a. salt
   b. raisins

5. a. tomato
   b. potatoes

6. a. pepper
   b. mushrooms

A.   Fill in the blanks.

Ex.   a _____quart_____
of milk

1.   a _____
of bananas

2.   a _____
of soup

3.   a _____
of onions

4.   a _____
of pie

5.   2 _____
of cereal

6.   2 _____
of bread

B.   Circle the correct answers.

Ex.   Yogurt (is) / are   cheap today.

1.   I eat too   much / many   cookies.

2.   She ate so   much / many   cake that

she has a stomachache.

3.   What do you   like / like to   do on the

weekend?

4.   How   much / many   does a bowl of

strawberries cost?

5.   Would you care for a   little / few   grapes?

I bought   it / them   this morning, and

it's / they're   very fresh.

6.   This / These   rice   is / are   delicious. May I

have a   little / few   more?

C.   Complete the sentences.

Ex.   Janet watches TV every Friday.

__She watched__   TV last Friday.

__She's going to watch__   TV next Friday.

1.   Alan drives to the mall every week.

He _____ to the mall last week.

_____

to the mall next week.

2.   I go on vacation every year.

I _____ on vacation last year.

_____

on vacation next year.

3. We play baseball every Saturday.

We _____ baseball last Saturday.

_____
baseball next Saturday.

4. My sister writes letters to her friends every weekend.

She _____ letters to her friends last weekend.

_____
letters to her friends next weekend.

5. Ed makes pancakes every morning.

He _____ pancakes yesterday morning.

_____
pancakes tomorrow morning.

D.   Complete the sentences.

Ex. Last year my parents gave me a sweater for my birthday.

This year ___*they're going to give me*___ a jacket.

1. Last year Tom gave his girlfriend flowers.

This year _____

_____ candy.

2. Last year Sue gave her husband a CD player.

This year _____

_____ a briefcase.

3. Last year we gave our parents a cell phone.

This year _____

_____ a computer.

E.   Listen and circle the correct word.

"I'm sorry, but there _____ any."

Ex. isn't
(aren't)

3. isn't
aren't

1. isn't
aren't

4. isn't
aren't

2. isn't
aren't

5. isn't
aren't

1. A. Will you be back soon?

   B. Yes, _____I will_____. _____I'll_____

   _____be back_____ in half an hour.

2. A. Will the game begin soon?

   B. Yes, _____. _____

   _____ in ten minutes.

3. A. Will Henry return soon?

   B. Yes, _____. _____

   _____ in a week.

4. A. Will we be ready soon?

   B. Yes, _____. _____

   _____ in a little while.

5. A. Will Grandma and Grandpa arrive soon?

   B. Yes, _____. _____

   _____ in 15 or 20 minutes.

6. A. Will the storm end soon?

   B. Yes, _____. _____

   _____ in a few hours.

7. A. Will Kate be here soon?

   B. Yes, _____. _____

   _____ in a few minutes.

8. A. Will you get out soon?

   B. Yes, _____. _____

   _____ in a month.

1. Do you think Barbara ___will___ move to a new apartment soon?

   I don't know. Maybe ___she___ ___will___, and maybe ___she___ ___won't___.

2. Do you think Robert _____ like his new job?

   I don't know. Maybe _____, and maybe _____.

3. Do you think _____ drive to the beach this weekend?

   I don't know. Maybe I _____, and maybe _____.

4. Do you think _____ be a famous scientist some day?

   I don't know. Maybe you _____, and maybe _____.

5. Do you think _____ snow a lot this winter?

   I don't know. Maybe _____, and maybe _____.

6. Do you think _____ _____ be a lot of traffic today?

   I don't know. Maybe _____, and maybe _____.

7. Do you think you and Roger _____ get married soon?

   I don't know. Maybe _____, and maybe _____.

8. Do you think the guests _____ like the fruitcake?

   I don't know. Maybe _____, and maybe _____.

C WHAT DO YOU THINK?

		Yes!	*No!*
1.	What will Charlie bake for the party?	Maybe _____he'll_____ _____bake_____ cookies.	I'm sure _____he_____ ___won't bake___ a cake.
2.	What will Mom order at the restaurant?	Maybe _____ _____ a sandwich.	I'm sure _____ _____ a pizza.
3.	Where will your parents go this evening?	Maybe _____ _____ to a movie.	I'm sure _____ _____ to a party.
4.	What will you get for your birthday?	Maybe _____ _____ a sweater.	I'm sure _____ _____ a cell phone.
5.	When will the train arrive?	Maybe _____ _____ in an hour.	I'm sure _____ _____ on time.
6.	When will we finish our English book?	Maybe _____ _____ it in a few months.	I'm sure _____ _____ it next week.

D LISTENING

Listen and circle the words you hear.

1.	won't / (want to)	3.	won't / want to	5.	won't / want to	7.	won't / want to
2.	won't / want to	4.	won't / want to	6.	won't / want to	8.	won't / want to

E DIFFERENT OPINIONS

1. I think the weather will be nice tomorrow. Everybody else thinks _____it 'll be_____ bad.

2. My wife thinks the guests will arrive on time. I think _____ late.

3. I think our daughter will be a lawyer. My husband thinks _____ an architect.

4. My parents think my brother Bob will buy a bicycle. I think _____ a motorcycle.

5. I think we'll have a good time at the party. My husband thinks _____ a terrible time.

F **GRAMMARRAP:** *You'll See*

Listen. Then clap and practice.

A.   I'll   remember.

B.   Are you   sure?

A.   Don't   worry.   I'll remember.   You'll see.

A.   He'll   do it.

B.   Are you   sure?

A.   Don't   worry.   He'll do it.   You'll see.

A.   She'll   call you.

B.   Are you   sure?

A.   Don't   worry.   She'll call you.   You'll see.

A.   It'll be   ready.

B.   Are you   sure?

A.   Don't   worry.   It'll be ready.   You'll see.

A.   We'll   be there.

B.   Are you   sure?

A.   Don't   worry.   We'll be there.   You'll see.

A.   They'll   get there.

B.   Are you   sure?

A.   Don't   worry.   They'll get there.   You'll see.

1. A. What's Bruno going to make for breakfast this morning?

   B. _____ He might make eggs _____ , or

   _____ he might make pancakes _____ .

2. A. What time is Sally going to get up tomorrow morning on her day off?

   B. _____ , or

   _____ .

3. A. When are your children going to clean their bedroom?

   B. _____ , or

   _____ .

4. A. What are you going to give your parents for their anniversary?

   B. _____ , or

   _____ .

5. A. What are you and your friends going to watch on TV tonight?

   B. _____ , or

   _____ .

6. A. Where are Mr. and Mrs. Martinez going to go for their vacation?

   B. _____ , or

   _____ .

7. A. Tell me, what are you going to do this weekend?

   B. _____ , or

   _____ .

8. A. What's Arthur going to name his new cat?

   B. _____ , or

   _____ .

H BE CAREFUL!

1. Don't stand there!
   (a.) You might get hit.
   b. You might watch.

2. Put on your safety glasses!
   a. You might hurt your ears.
   b. You might hurt your eyes.

3. Don't touch those wires!
   a. You might get a shock.
   b. You might get cold.

4. Don't touch that machine!
   a. You might get hurt.
   b. You might get a helmet.

5. Watch your step!
   a. You might finish.
   b. You might fall.

6. Put on your helmet!
   a. You might hurt your back.
   b. You might hurt your head.

I LOUD AND CLEAR

W!

| winter   Wendy   walk   weather   work |

1. ____Wendy____ doesn't like to ____walk____
   to ____work____ in the ____winter____ when
   the ____weather____ is bad.

| wet   walk   waiter   won't   waitress |

2. The _____ and the _____
   _____ _____ there. The floor is
   _____!

| wife   wash   Walter   windows   want   weekend |

3. _____ and his _____
   _____ to _____ their
   _____ this _____.

| wasn't   we   water   wanted   warm |

4. _____ _____ to go
   swimming, but the _____
   _____ _____.

break her leg	fall asleep	get fat	have a terrible time	rain
catch a cold	get a backache	get seasick	look terrible	step on her feet
drown	get a sunburn	get sick	miss our bus	

1. Jennifer won't go skating because

   she's afraid she might

   break her leg .

2. George won't go to the beach because

   _____

   _____ .

3. I won't go swimming because

   _____

   _____ .

4. We won't have lunch with you because

   _____

   _____ .

5. My mother and father won't go on the roller

   coaster because _____

   _____ .

6. Brian won't go dancing with Brenda

   because _____

   _____ .

7. We won't go to a play because

   _____

   _____ .

8. I won't go to Patty's party because

   _____

   _____ .

9. Barry won't carry those boxes because

_____

_____.

10. Sally won't go sailing because

_____

_____.

11. I won't eat dessert because

_____

_____.

12. Helen won't take a walk in the park because

_____

_____.

13. We won't wash our clothes today because

_____

_____.

14. Fred won't get a short haircut because

_____

_____.

K **LISTENING**

Listen and choose the correct answer.

1. a. He doesn't want to go on the roller coaster.
b. He doesn't want to go to the doctor.

2. a. She doesn't want to go skiing.
b. She doesn't want to go to the movies.

3. a. He doesn't want to go to a play.
b. He doesn't want to go dancing.

4. a. She doesn't want to go skiing.
b. She doesn't want to stay home.

5. a. He doesn't want to read a book.
b. He doesn't want to take a walk in the park.

6. a. He doesn't want to go swimming.
b. He doesn't want to go dancing.

7. a. She doesn't want to go skating.
b. She doesn't want to go sailing.

8. a. He doesn't want to go to the library.
b. He doesn't want to go to the beach.

9. a. She doesn't want to go to the party.
b. She doesn't want to eat dinner.

10. a. He doesn't want to get a short haircut.
b. He doesn't want to buy a small dog.

L **GRAMMARRAP:** *He Might*

Listen. Then clap and practice.

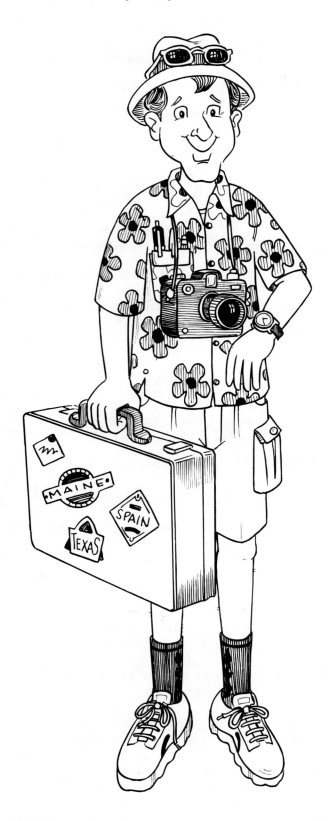

A. When is he going to   leave?

B. He might leave at   noon.

C. He might leave on   Monday.

D. He might leave in   June.

A. Where is he going to   go?

B. He might go to   Spain.

C. He might go to   Texas.

D. He might go to   Maine.

A. How is he going to   get there?

B. He might go by   train.

C. He might take the   bus.

D. He might take a   plane.

A. Who is he going to   go with?

B. He might go with   Ed.

C. He might go with   Peter.

D. He might go with   Fred.

A. What's he going to   do there?

B. He might see the   zoo.

C. He might take some   pictures.

D. He might write to   you.

M GRAMMARSONG: *We Really Can't Decide*

Listen and fill in the words to the song. Then listen again and sing along.

cake	decide	go	her	make	Mexico	sweater	wide

I want to cook some dinner.

I don't know what to ___**make**___ 1.

I might make stew. I might make eggs.

I might just bake a _____ 2.

I really don't know what to cook.

The choices are so _____ 3.

I might cook this. I might cook that.

I really can't _____ 4.

I'm planning my vacation.

I don't know where to _____ 5.

I might see France. I might see Spain.

I might see _____ 6.

I really don't know where to go.

The choices are so _____ 7.

I might go here. I might go there.

I really can't _____ 8.

I'm buying Mom a present.

I don't know what to get _____ 9.

I might buy gloves. I might buy boots.

I might get her a _____ 10.

I really don't know what to get.

The choices are so _____ 11.

I might get this. I might get that.

I really can't _____ 12.

Activity Workbook   **39**

A OLD AND NEW

1. Henry's old sofa was soft. His new sofa is _____softer_____.

2. Nancy's old briefcase was light. Her new briefcase is _____.

3. Bob's old living room was large. His new living room is _____.

4. My old recipe for chili was hot. My new recipe is _____.

5. My old boss was friendly. My new boss is _____.

6. Our old neighborhood was safe. Our new neighborhood is _____.

7. Linda's old cell phone was small. Her new cell phone is _____.

8. Grandpa's old sports car was fancy. His new sports car is _____.

9. Cathy's old mittens were warm. Her new mittens are _____.

10. Billy's old school was big. His new school is _____.

11. My old job was easy. My new job is _____.

12. Our old neighbors were nice. Our new neighbors are _____.

13. Richard's old watch was cheap. His new watch is _____.

14. Dr. Green's old office was ugly. His new office is _____.

B WHAT'S THE WORD?

1. A. Is Tim's hair short?

   B. Yes, but Jim's hair is _____shorter_____.

2. A. Is Charlie's cat cute?

   B. Yes, but his dog is _____.

3. A. Is Debbie's dog fat?

   B. Yes, but her cat is _____.

4. A. Is Barbara busy?

   B. Yes, but Betty is _____.

40   Activity Workbook

C THEY'RE DIFFERENT

1. Paul's parrot is talkative, but Paula's parrot is _____ more talkative _____.

2. Your roommate is interesting, but my roommate is _____.

3. Sam's suit is attractive, but Stanley's suit is _____.

4. Shirley's shoes are comfortable, but her sister's shoes are _____.

5. George is intelligent, but his brother is _____.

6. My daughter's hair is long, but my son's hair is _____.

7. Last winter was cold, but this winter is _____.

8. William is thin, but his father is _____.

9. My children are healthy, but my doctor's children are _____.

10. John's computer is powerful, but Jane's computer is _____.

11. Barbara's boyfriend is handsome, but her father is _____.

12. My teeth are white, but my dentist's teeth are _____.

13. Our neighbor's yard is beautiful, but our yard is _____.

D WHAT'S THE WORD?

1. A. This meatloaf is delicious.
   B. It's very good, but my mother's meatloaf

   is _____ more delicious _____.

2. A. Chicken is good for you.
   B. I know. But everybody says that fish

   is _____ for you.

3. A. This necklace is very expensive.
   B. You're right. But that necklace

   is _____.

4. A. You're very energetic!
   B. Yes, I am. But my wife is _____

   _____.

Across

4. My upstairs neighbor is friendly, but my downstairs neighbor is _____.
7. Their baby is cute, but my baby is   .
8. Betty's blue dress is pretty, but her green dress is   .
11. This bicycle is fast, but that bicycle is   .
12. My old apartment was large, but my new apartment is   .
13. Your dishwasher is quiet, but my dishwasher is   .

Down

1. Our old rug was soft, but our new rug is   .
2. Yesterday it was warm, but today it's   .
3. Their new house is small, but their old house was   .
4. Tom's new tie is fancy, but his son's tie is   .
5. My old tennis racket was light, but my new tennis racket is   .
6. Bananas were cheap last week, but this week they're   .
9. The chili we ate last week was hot, but this chili is   .
10. This picture is ugly, but that picture is   .

F **LISTENING**

Listen and choose the correct words to complete the sentences.

1. a. cooler
   b. cuter

2. a. smaller
   b. taller

3. a. more handsome
   b. more attractive

4. a. nicer
   b. lighter

5. a. fatter
   b. faster

6. a. friendlier
   b. fancier

7. a. more interesting
   b. more intelligent

8. a. bigger
   b. busier

G LET'S COMPARE!

cheap	delicious	fancy	small	talented	talkative

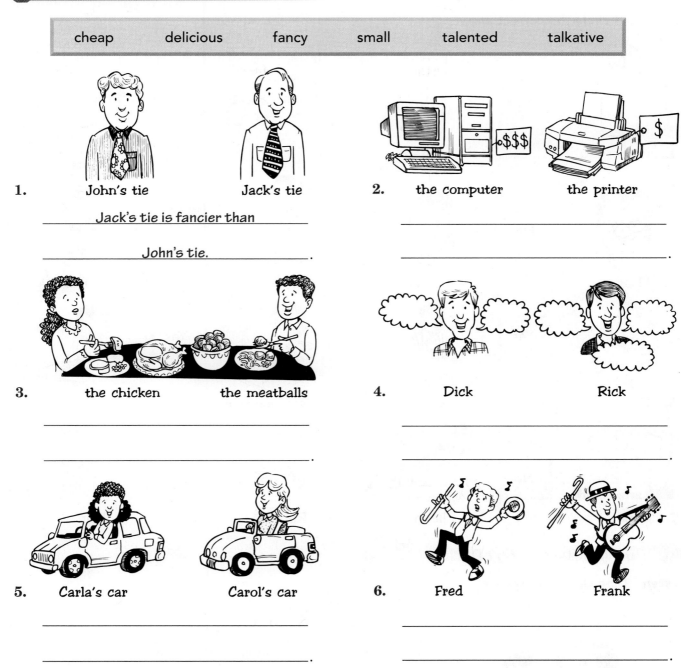

1. John's tie   Jack's tie

_____Jack's tie is fancier than_____

_____John's tie._____ .

2. the computer   the printer

_____

_____ .

3. the chicken   the meatballs

_____

_____ .

4. Dick   Rick

_____

_____ .

5. Carla's car   Carol's car

_____

_____ .

6. Fred   Frank

_____

_____ .

H GRAMMARRAP: *Honey Is Sweeter Than Sugar*

Listen. Then clap and practice.

Honey is	sweeter than	sugar.		Peaches are	softer than	apples.
Coffee is	stronger than	tea.		Pepper is	hotter than	rice.
Hours are	longer than	minutes.		Pears are	bigger than	lemons.
Thirty is	larger than three.			Nothing is	colder than	ice.

Activity Workbook   43

I LISTENING

Listen and circle the correct answer.

1. yesterday / today **(Yes)** No

2. $2.50 / $3.25 — Yes / No

3. Betty / Jane — Yes / No

4. Bob / Bill — Yes / No

5. Barry / Larry — Yes / No

6. science test / history test — Yes / No

7. Irene / Eileen — Yes / No

8. Ronald / Donald — Yes / No

J GRAMMARRAP: *I Can't Decide*

Listen. Then clap and practice.

I can't decide   who to go   out with.
Bob is more   interesting than   Bill.
Tom is more   handsome than   Tony.
And Frank's more   exciting than   Phil.

I can't decide   who to go   out with.
Alice is more   talented than   Anne.
Sue's more   attractive than   Sally.
And Jane's more   exciting than   Jan.

44   Activity Workbook

K WHAT SHOULD THEY DO?

| call the dentist | fire him | rent a video |
| call the police | hire her | plant some flowers |

1. My garden looks terrible!

___You should plant some flowers.___

2. Harvey has a very bad toothache!

_____

3. My husband and I want to see a movie tonight.

_____

4. A thief stole my daughter's new bicycle!

_____

5. The people at the Ace company think that Jennifer is capable and talented.

_____

6. Ms. Hunter is upset because her secretary falls asleep at work every day.

_____

L GRAMMARRAP: *Should They...?*

Listen. Then clap and practice.

A. Should he   call or should he   write?

B. He should   call   tomorrow   night.

A. Should I   keep it or give it   back?

B. You should wear it or give it to   Jack.

A. Should I   stay or   should I   go?

B. Don't ask me.   I don't   know.

Activity Workbook **45**

1. Should I buy a van or a sports car?

   I think _you should buy a van_   I think _you should buy a sports car_
   because _vans are more useful than_   *(or)*   because _sports cars are more_
   sports cars .   _exciting than vans_ .

   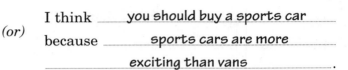

2. Should she buy a bicycle or a motorcycle?   3. Should we move to Weston or Easton?

   I think _____   I think _____
   because _____   because _____

   _____ .   _____ .

4. Should he buy the fur hat or the leather hat? 5. Should I vote for Alan Lane or George Gray?

   I think _____   I think _____
   because _____   because _____

   _____ .   _____ .

6. Should we hire Mr. Hall or Mr. Hill?   7. Should he go out with Patty or Pam?

   I think _____   I think _____
   because _____   because _____

   _____ .   _____ .

N WHAT'S THE WORD?

mine	his	hers	ours	yours	theirs

1. A. Is this Michael's cell phone?

   B. No. It isn't _____his_____.

2. A. Are these your safety glasses?

   B. No. They aren't _____.

3. A. Is this your sister's violin?

   B. No. It isn't _____.

4. A. Is that Mr. and Mrs. Garcia's van?

   B. No. It isn't _____.

5. A. Is this my recipe for fruitcake?

   B. No. It isn't _____.

6. A. Are these your son's sneakers?

   B. No. They aren't _____.

7. Is that your car?

   No. It isn't _____.

O WHAT'S THE WORD?

1. You know, my parents aren't as sympathetic as your parents.

   Really? I think ((yours) your) are much more sympathetic than (my mine).

2. Robert's cookies aren't as delicious as his sister's cookies.

   Really? I think (him his) are much more delicious than (her hers).

3. Our computer isn't as fast as their computer.

   Really? I think (ours their) is much faster than (theirs them).

4. My pronunciation isn't as good as your pronunciation.

   Don't be ridiculous! (Your Yours) is much better than (mine my).

5. Jane's briefcase isn't as attractive as her husband's briefcase.

   Really? I think (her hers) is much more attractive than (him his).

Activity Workbook   **47**

P DIFFERENT, BUT OKAY

1. My neighborhood (quiet) _____ isn't as quiet as _____ your neighborhood, but it's

   much (interesting) _____ more interesting _____.

2. Susan's sofa (fashionable) _____ her sister's sofa, but it's

   much (comfortable) _____.

3. These apartments (modern) _____ our apartment, but

   they're much (large) _____.

4. George's car (powerful) _____ Jack's car, but it's much

   (reliable) _____.

5. The weather in our city (warm) _____ the weather in your

   city, but it's much (sunny) _____.

6. My parents (talkative) _____ my cousin's parents, but

   they're much (understanding) _____.

7. The movie we rented last weekend wasn't (exciting) _____

   this movie, but it was much (good) _____.

Q YOU'RE RIGHT

1. A. Ken's tie isn't as attractive as Len's tie.

   B. You're right. Len's tie is _____ more _____

   _____ attractive than Ken's tie _____.

2. A. Donald isn't as nice as Ronald.

   B. You're right. Ronald is _____

   _____.

3. A. Larry isn't as lazy as his brother.

   B. You're right. Larry's brother is _____

   _____.

4. A. English isn't as difficult as Russian.

   B. You're right. Russian is _____

   _____.

5. A. Julie's office isn't as big as Judy's office.

   B. You're right. Judy's office is _____

   _____.

6. A. My son isn't as talkative as your son.

   B. You're right. My son is _____

   _____.

Listen. Then clap and practice.

Where's my ticket?
Who has mine?
I don't want to
stand in line.

Who has hers?
Who has his?
I wonder where
my ticket is!

He has his.
I have mine.
She has hers.
Everything's fine!

S **GRAMMARRAP:** *His Job Is Easy*

Listen. Then clap and practice.

His job is easy.
Hers is, too.
Mine's a more difficult job to do.
His job's as simple
As A B C.
Mine requires a P H D.

T WHO SHOULD WE HIRE?

A. Do you think we should hire Mr. Blake or Mr. Maxwell?

B. I'm not sure. Mr. Blake isn't as (lively) _____lively_____ 1

as Mr. Maxwell, but he's much (smart) _____ 2.

A. I agree. Mr. Blake is very smart, but in my opinion,

Mr. Maxwell is (talented) _____ 3 than
Mr. Blake.

B. Well, perhaps Mr. Blake isn't as (talented) _____ 4 as

Mr. Maxwell, but I think he's probably (honest) _____ 5.

A. Do you really think so?

B. Yes. I think Mr. Blake is much (good) _____ 6 for the job.
We should hire him.

A. Do you think we should hire Ms. Taylor or Ms. Tyler?

B. I'm not sure. Ms. Tyler isn't as (friendly) _____ 7

as Ms. Taylor, but I think she's much (intelligent) _____

_____ 8.

A. But Ms. Taylor is (talkative) _____ 9

and (polite) _____ 10 than Ms. Tyler.

B. That's true. But I think Ms. Tyler is (capable) _____

_____ 11 than Ms. Taylor. I think we should hire her.

A. Do you think we should hire Mario or Victor?

B. I don't know. Mario's meatballs are (good) _____ 12

than Victor's, but his desserts aren't as (delicious)

_____ 13 as Victor's desserts.

A. That's true. But Mario's vegetable stew is (interesting)

_____ 14 than Victor's. Also, Mario is

much (fast) _____ 15 than Victor. He's also

(nice) _____ 16 than Victor.

B. You're right. I think we should hire Mario.

50   Activity Workbook

1. A. I think Alice is very bright.

   B. She certainly is. She's ___the___
      ___brightest___ student in our class.

2. A. Your brother Tom is very neat.

   B. He certainly is. He's _____
      _____ person I know.

3. A. Our upstairs neighbors are very nice.

   B. I agree. They're _____
      people in the building.

4. A. This dress is very fancy.

   B. I know. It's _____
      dress in the store.

5. A. I think Nancy is very friendly.

   B. I agree. She's _____
      person in our office.

6. A. Timothy is very quiet.

   B. I know. He's _____
      boy in the school.

7. A. Is their new baby cute?

   B. In my opinion, she's _____
      _____ baby girl in
      the hospital.

8. A. That dog is very big.

   B. It certainly is. It's _____
      _____ dog in the
      neighborhood.

9. A. Your cousin Steven is very sloppy.

   B. He certainly is. He's _____
      _____ person I know.

10. A. Morton Miller is very mean.

    B. I agree. He's _____
       _____ man in town.

| boring | generous | interesting | patient | smart | talented |
| energetic | honest | noisy | polite | stubborn | |

1. Jessica sings, dances, and plays the guitar. She's very _____ talented _____.

   In fact, she's _____ the most talented _____ person I know.

2. Mr. Bates gives very expensive gifts to his friends. He's very _____.

   In fact, he's _____ person I know.

3. My Aunt Louise jogs every day before work. She's very _____.

   In fact, she's _____ person I know.

4. Marvin always says "Thank you" and "You're welcome." He's very _____.

   In fact, he's _____ person I know.

5. Samantha always knows the answers to all the questions. She's very _____.

   In fact, she's _____ person I know.

6. Edward isn't reading a very exciting novel. It's very _____.

   In fact, it's _____ book in his house.

7. Dr. Chen never gets angry. She's very _____.

   In fact, she's _____ person I know.

8. Mayor Jones always says what he thinks. He's very _____.

   In fact, he's _____ person I know.

9. My next-door neighbor plays loud music after midnight. He's very _____.

   In fact, he's _____ person I know.

10. I'm never bored in my English class. My English teacher is very _____.

    In fact, she's _____ person I know.

11. My brother-in-law is always sure he's right. He's very _____.

    In fact, he's _____ person I know.

WorldBuy.com is a very popular website on the Internet. People like to shop there because they can find wonderful products from around the world at very low prices.

1. *(attractive!)* Julie is buying a briefcase from Italy because she thinks that Italian briefcases are _____ the most attractive _____ briefcases in the world.

2. *(soft!)* David is buying leather boots from Spain because he thinks that Spanish boots are _____ boots in the world.

3. *(elegant!)* Francine is buying an evening gown from Paris because she thinks that French evening gowns are _____ gowns in the world.

4. *(modern!)* Mr. and Mrs. Chang are buying a sofa from Sweden because they think that Swedish furniture is _____ furniture in the world.

5. *(warm!)* Victor is buying a fur hat from Russia because he thinks that Russian hats are _____ hats in the world.

6. *(good!)* Brenda is buying a sweater from England because she thinks that English sweaters are _____ sweaters in the world.

7. *(reliable!)* Michael is buying a watch from Switzerland because he thinks that Swiss watches are _____ watches in the world.

8. *(beautiful!)* Mr. and Mrs. Rivera are buying a rug from China because they think that Chinese rugs are _____ rugs in the world.

9. *(delicious!)* Nancy is buying coffee from Brazil because she thinks that Brazilian coffee is _____ in the world.

10. *(_____ !)* I'm buying _____ from _____ because I think that _____ _____ s is/are _____ in the world.

D GRAMMARRAP: *What Do You Think About . . . ?*

Listen. Then clap and practice.

A. What do you think about Kirk?
B. He's the friendliest person at work!

A. What do you think about Flo?
B. She's the most patient person I know!

A. What do you think about Pete?
B. He's the nicest boy on the street!

A. What do you think about Kate?
B. She's the most talented teacher in the state!

A. What do you think about Bob?
B. He's the laziest guy on the job!

A. What do you think about Frank?
B. He's the most polite teller at the bank!

A. What do you think about Nellie?
B. She's the fastest waitress at the deli!

A. What do you think about this kitty?
B. It's the ugliest cat in the city!

1. A. How do you like your new BMB van, Mr. Lopez?

    B. It's very powerful. It's much ____more____

        _____powerful_____ than my old van.

    A. That's because the BMB van is _____

        _____the most powerful_____ van in the world!

2. A. How do you like your Suny video camera, Mrs. Park?

    B. It's very lightweight. It's much _____

        _____ than my old video camera.

    A. That's because the Suny video camera is _____

        _____ video camera in the world!

3. A. How do you like your new Inkflo printer, Ted?

    B. It's very efficient. It's much _____

        _____ than my old printer.

    A. That's because the Inkflo printer is _____

        _____ printer in the world!

4. A. How do you like your Panorama fax machine, Jane?

    B. It's very dependable. It's much _____

        _____ than my old fax machine.

    A. That's because the Panorama fax machine is _____

        _____ fax machine in the world!

5. A. How do you like your new Ever-Lite Flashlight, Henry?

    B. It's very bright. It's much _____ than the
        flashlight I usually use.

    A. That's because the Ever-Lite Flashlight is _____

        _____ flashlight in the world!

LISTENING

Listen and circle the words you hear.

1. (more comfortable)   the most comfortable   6. sloppier   the sloppiest

2. the best   the worst   7. the worst   the best

3. more energetic   the most energetic   8. lazier   lazy

4. cheap   cheaper   9. meaner   mean

5. the most important   more important   10. more honest   the most honest

G **PUZZLE**

boring   comfortable   delicious   good   honest   polite   safe   sloppy   small   ugly

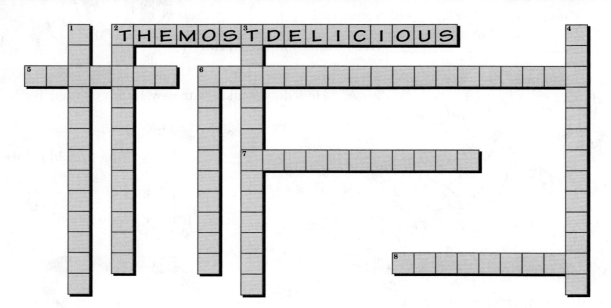

Across

2. Some people don't like this cereal. But I disagree. I think it's _____ cereal in the world.

5. Even though Harry's Restaurant is the most popular restaurant in town, it isn't _____.

6. This is my favorite chair. That's because it's _____ chair in the house.

7. My house isn't very big. In fact, it's _____ house on the street.

8. Their old neighborhood was dangerous, but their new neighborhood is _____ neighborhood in the city.

Down

1. Even though the salespeople at Ace Used Cars are the most helpful in town, they aren't _____.

2. My son isn't very neat. In my opinion, he's _____ person in our family.

3. I think golf is very interesting. But my wife disagrees. She thinks it's _____ game in the world.

4. Charles is never rude. In fact, he's _____ boy in the school.

6. Emily's cat isn't very pretty. In my opinion, it's _____ cat in town!

H LOUD AND CLEAR r!

Fill in the words. Then read the sentences aloud.

worst	program	Andrew
terrible		actor

1. ___Andrew___ is the ___worst___
    ___actor___ on this ___terrible___
    TV ___program___!

recipe	Carla's	fruitcake
recommend		better

2. I _____ _____
    _____ for _____.
    It's _____ than yours.

energetic	friendlier	Robert
more		brother

3. _____ is _____
    and _____ _____
    than his _____ Richard.

newspaper	writes	reads
Rita		morning

4. _____ _____ the _____
    every _____, and she
    _____ letters every afternoon.

perfume	birthday	sister
Ronald		thirtieth

5. _____ gave his _____
    flowers and _____ for her
    _____ _____.

powerful	bigger	more
neighbor's		car

6. My _____ is _____ and
    _____ _____ than my
    _____ car.

✔ CHECK-UP TEST: Chapters 4–6

A. Complete the sentences.

Ex. Will you be ready soon?

Yes, __I will__. __I'll__ be ready in a few minutes.

Ex. Will your brother get home soon?

No, __he won't__. He's at a baseball game tonight.

1. Will the storm end soon?

Yes, _____. _____ end in a few hours.

2. Will Carol and Dave be in the office today?

No, _____. They're on vacation.

3. Will you return soon?

Yes, _____. _____ return in a little while.

4. Will Jane be in school tomorrow?

No, _____. She has a bad cold.

5. Will you and Ray get out of work soon?

Yes, _____. _____ get out in half an hour.

B. Circle the correct answers.

1. I'm not going to fix that wire. I'm afraid I might / should get a shock.

2. What do you think? Might / Should I order the chicken or the fish?

3. When I grow up I might / should be a dentist, or I might / should be a doctor.

4. It's going to rain. You might / should take your umbrella.

C. Complete the conversations.

Ex. A. Are these Maria's gloves?

B. No. They aren't __hers__.

1. A. Is that your video camera?

B. No. It isn't _____.

2. A. Is that your son's computer?

B. No. It isn't _____.

3. A. Is that Mr. and Mrs. Baker's house?

B. No. It isn't _____.

4. A. Is this my recipe for meatballs?

B. No. It isn't _____.

D. Fill in the blanks.

Ex. Donald is __neater than__ Sam.
     neat

1. Jane is _____ Sarah.
   tall

2. Carl is _____ Jack.
   honest

3. Centerville is _____ Lakeville.
   pretty

4. The pie is _____ the cake.
   good

5. Julie is _____ John.
   dependable

E. Complete the sentences.

Ex. William (rich) _____isn't as_____

_____rich as_____ Walter, but he's

much (happy) _____happier_____.

1. Ann's printer (fast) _____

   _____ Betty's printer, but it's much

   (reliable) _____.

2. Danny's dog (friendly) _____

   _____ Dorothy's dog, but it's much

   (cute) _____.

3. Howard (intelligent) _____

   _____ Mike, but he's much (interesting)

   _____.

4. My apartment (fashionable) _____

   _____ your

   apartment, but it's much (big)

   _____.

5. Tom's furniture (expensive) _____

   _____ John's

   furniture, but it's much (attractive)

   _____.

F. Fill in the blanks.

Ex. Brian is _____the smartest_____ person
                        smart
I know.

1. Marvin is _____ person
                        quiet
I know.

2. Uncle Bert is _____
                        hospitable
person in our family.

3. We have _____
                        large
apartment in the building.

4. Mr. Peterson is _____
                        patient
teacher in our school.

5. Mel is _____ person
                        lazy
I know.

G. Listen and circle the correct answer.

Ex. Ronald   (Yes) / No   Fred

1. Bob   Yes / No   Bill

    $6/lb.   Yes / No $4/lb.

2.

   Moscow 32°   Yes / No   Miami 90°

3. Moscow   Miami

4. Herbert   Yes / No   Steven

5. Pam   Yes / No    Patty

A HOW DO I GET THERE?

across from	on the right	walk up
between	on the left	walk down
next to		

7

SOUTH ST.

barber shop	library
clinic	toy store
shoe store	post office
bakery	book store
bank	drug store
high school	police station

1. A. Excuse me. Can you tell me how to get to the library from here?

   B. __Walk up__ South Street and you'll see the library __on the right__, __across from__ the barber shop.

2. A. Excuse me. Can you tell me how to get to the clinic from here?

   B. _____ South Street and you'll see the clinic _____, _____ the shoe store.

3. A. Excuse me. Can you tell me how to get to the toy store from here?

   B. _____ South Street and you'll see the toy store _____, _____ the clinic.

4. A. Excuse me. Can you tell me how to get to the drug store from here?

   B. _____ South Street and you'll see the drug store _____, _____ the book store and the police station.

5. A. Excuse me. Can you tell me how to get to the high school from here?

   B. _____ South Street and you'll see the high school _____, _____ the bank and _____ the police station.

B WHICH WAY?

across from
between
next to
on the left
on the right

walk along
walk down
walk up

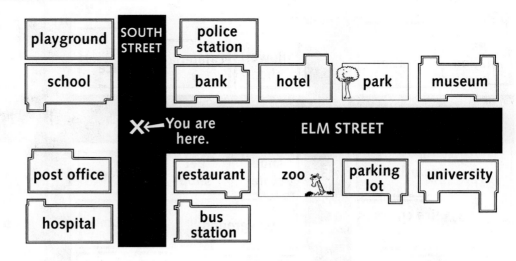

1. A. Excuse me. Could you please tell me how to get to the university from here?

   B. ____Walk along____ Elm Street and you'll see the university

   ____on the right____, ____across from____ the museum.

2. A. Excuse me. Could you please tell me how to get to the park from here?

   B. _____ Elm Street and you'll see the park

   _____, _____ the hotel.

3. A. Excuse me. Could you please tell me how to get to the police station from here?

   B. _____ South Street and you'll see the police station

   _____, _____ the playground.

4. A. Excuse me. Could you please tell me how to get to the bus station from here?

   B. _____ South Street and you'll see the bus station

   _____, _____ the restaurant.

5. A. Excuse me. Could you please tell me how to get to the zoo from here?

   B. _____ Elm Street and you'll see the zoo

   _____, _____ the restaurant and
   the parking lot.

Map labels: playground, SOUTH STREET, police station, school, bank, hotel, park, museum, X ←You are here., ELM STREET, post office, restaurant, zoo, parking lot, university, hospital, bus station

Activity Workbook 61

C LET'S HELP MR. AND MRS. LEE!

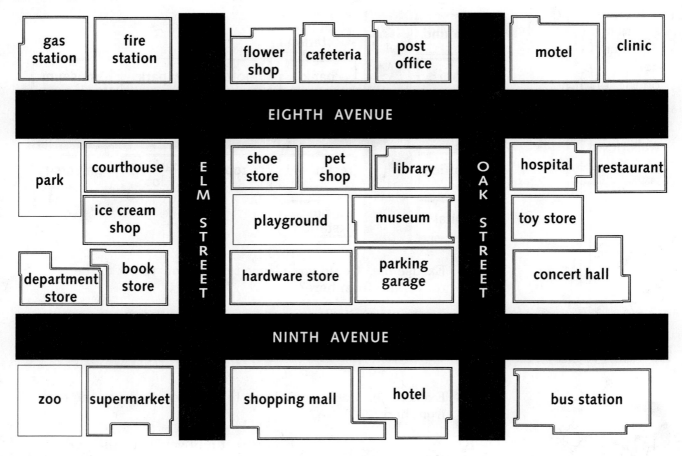

| gas station | fire station | | flower shop | cafeteria | post office | | motel | clinic |

EIGHTH AVENUE

park	courthouse		shoe store	pet shop	library		hospital	restaurant
	ice cream shop	E L M S T R E E T	playground	museum		O A K S T R E E T	toy store
department store	book store		hardware store	parking garage			concert hall

NINTH AVENUE

| zoo | supermarket | | shopping mall | hotel | | bus station |

Mr. and Mrs. Lee are very busy today. They want to go several places with their children, but they don't know the city very well. They need your help.

1. They're at the shopping mall, and they want to take their children to the toy store to buy them a new toy. Tell them how to get there.

_____Walk along_____ Ninth Avenue to Oak Street and _____turn left_____. _____Walk up_____ Oak Street and you'll see the toy store _____on the right_____, _____across from_____ the museum.

2. They're at the toy store, and now they want to take their children to the pet shop to buy them a dog.

_____ Oak Street to Eighth Avenue and _____. _____ Eighth Avenue and you'll see the pet shop _____, _____ the shoe store and the library.

3. They're at the pet shop, and they want to take their children to the ice cream shop for some ice cream.

_____ Eighth Avenue to Elm Street and

_____. _____ Elm Street

and you'll see the ice cream shop _____,

_____ the courthouse.

4. They're at the ice cream shop, and they want to take their children to the zoo.

_____ Elm Street to Ninth Avenue and

_____. _____ Ninth

Avenue and you'll see the zoo _____,

_____ the department store.

5. They're at the zoo, and they're tired. They want to go to the park to rest.

6. They had a wonderful day, and now it's time to go home. Tell them how to get to the bus station.

D LISTENING

Look at the map on page 62. Listen and choose the correct answer.

1. a. She was hungry.
   b. She wanted to buy a bird.

2. a. He wanted to look at paintings.
   b. He wanted to listen to music.

3. a. They wanted to read some books.
   b. They wanted to buy some flowers.

4. a. She wanted to buy some toys for her son.
   b. She wanted to visit her sick friend.

5. a. He wanted to buy some groceries.
   b. He wanted to look at the animals.

6. a. She was sick.
   b. She was hungry.

Listen. Then clap and practice.

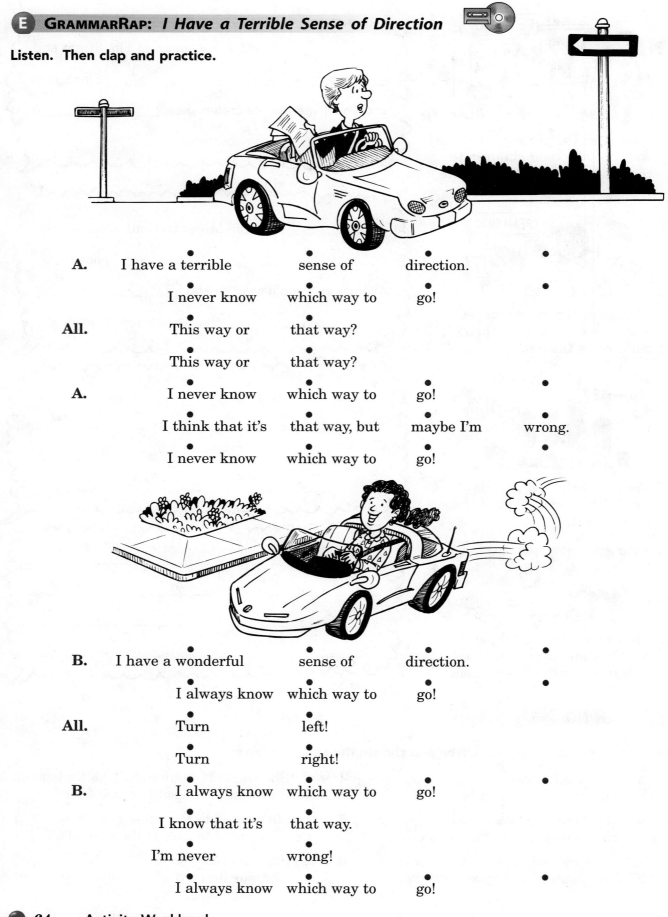

A.   I have a terrible   sense of   direction.
         I never know   which way to   go!

All.   This way or   that way?
           This way or   that way?

A.   I never know   which way to   go!
         I think that it's   that way, but   maybe I'm   wrong.
         I never know   which way to   go!

B.   I have a wonderful   sense of   direction.
         I always know   which way to   go!

All.   Turn   left!
           Turn   right!

B.   I always know   which way to   go!
         I know that it's   that way.
         I'm never   wrong!
         I always know   which way to   go!

F IN A HURRY!

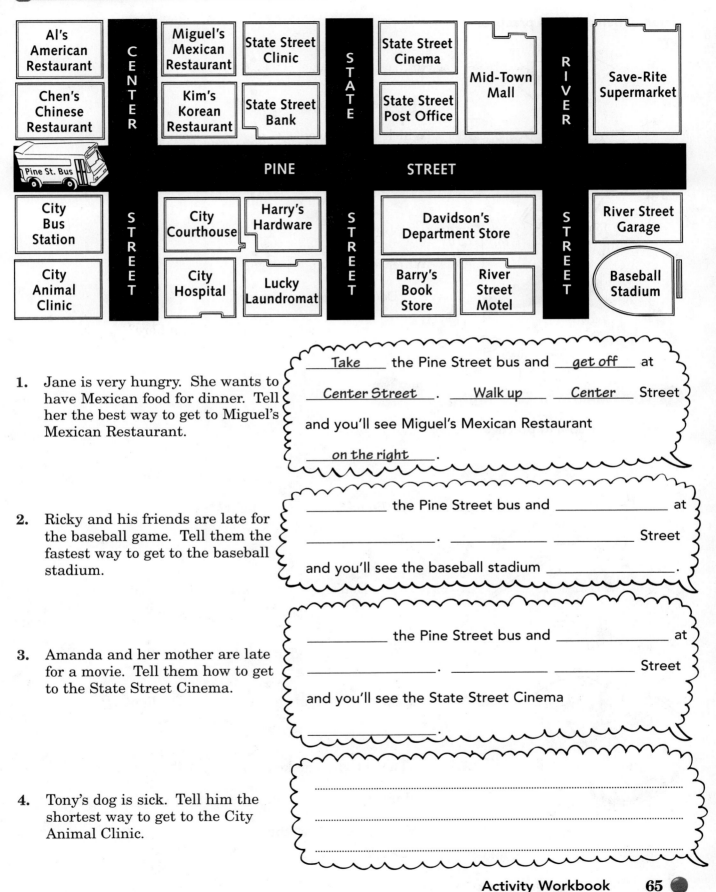

1. Jane is very hungry. She wants to have Mexican food for dinner. Tell her the best way to get to Miguel's Mexican Restaurant.

    __Take__ the Pine Street bus and __get off__ at __Center Street__ . __Walk up__ __Center__ Street and you'll see Miguel's Mexican Restaurant __on the right__ .

2. Ricky and his friends are late for the baseball game. Tell them the fastest way to get to the baseball stadium.

    _____ the Pine Street bus and _____ at _____ . _____ _____ Street and you'll see the baseball stadium _____ .

3. Amanda and her mother are late for a movie. Tell them how to get to the State Street Cinema.

    _____ the Pine Street bus and _____ at _____ . _____ _____ Street and you'll see the State Street Cinema _____ .

4. Tony's dog is sick. Tell him the shortest way to get to the City Animal Clinic.

G GRAMMARRAP: *Which Way Do We Go?*

Listen. Then clap and practice.

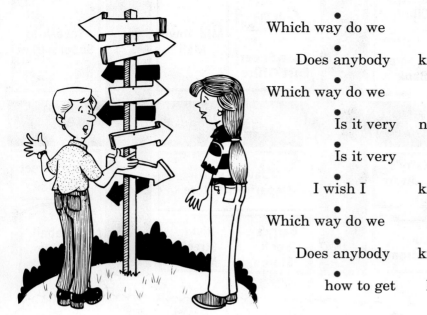

Which way do we go?

Does anybody know?

Which way do we go from here?

Is it very near?

Is it very far?

I wish I knew where I left my car!

Which way do we go?

Does anybody know

how to get home from here?

H GRAMMARRAP: *Turn Right!*

Listen. Then clap and practice.

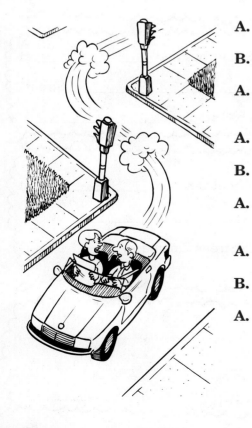

A. Turn right at the next light.

B. At the next light?

A. That's right.

A. Don't turn left! Turn right!

B. At the light?

A. That's right. Turn right at the light.

A. Make a left at the next light.

B. Make a left?

A. That's right, make a left at the light.

Make a left at the light and then turn right.

Make a left at the next light.

I LISTENING: *Where Did They Go?*

```
                           DAY STREET
┌─────────────────────┐ F ┌──────────────────────┐ S ┌──────────────────────┐ T
│   shopping mall     │ I │       museum         │ E │       hospital       │ H
├────────┬──────┬─────┤ R ├────────┬──────┬──────┤ C ├────────┬───────┬─────┤ I
│        │ bus  │     │ S │  ice   │      │      │ O │ high   │ post  │     │ R
│ bakery │station│hotel│ T │ cream  │motel │clinic│ N │ school │office │park │ D
│        │      │     │   │ shop   │      │      │ D │        │       │     │
└────────┴──────┴─────┘   └────────┴──────┴──────┘   └────────┴───────┴─────┘
                        BRIGHTON BOULEVARD
┌────────┬──────┬─────┐ S ┌────────┬──────┬──────┐ S ┌────────┬───────┬─────┐ S
│ barber │ book │drug │ T │parking │ toy  │ gas  │ E │police  │       │ pet │ T
│ shop   │store │store│ R │  lot   │store │station│ C │station │ bank  │shop │ R
├────────┴──────┴─────┤ E ├────────┼──────┼──────┤ O ├────────┼───────┼─────┤ E
│concert │          │ E │flower  │      │      │ N │ shoe   │parking│fire │ E
│  hall  │   zoo    │ T │ shop   │library│church│ D │ store  │garage │station│ T
└────────┴──────────┘   └────────┴──────┴──────┘   └────────┴───────┴─────┘
                           BAY AVENUE
```

Listen and fill in the correct places.

1. He went to the _____bank_____.

2. She went to the _____.

3. They went to the _____.

4. She went to the _____.

5. They went to the _____.

6. He went to the _____.

J WHAT'S THE WORD?

between	could	from	how	off	subway	turn	walk
certainly	excuse	get	left	please	take	up	

A. ___Excuse___ ¹ me. _____ ² you _____ ³

tell me _____ ⁴ to _____ ⁵ to the train

station _____ ⁶ here?

B. _____ ⁷. _____ ⁸ the

_____ ⁹ and get _____ ¹⁰ at Park Street.

Walk _____ ¹¹ Park Street to Tenth Avenue

and _____ ¹² right. _____ ¹³ along Tenth

Avenue and you'll see the train station on the

_____ ¹⁴, _____ ¹⁵ the post office
and the fire station.

APPENDIX

Activity Workbook Listening Scripts

Page 2 Exercise B

Listen and choose the correct response.

1. What do your friends like to do on the weekend?
2. What does your sister like to do on the weekend?
3. What does your brother like to do on the weekend?
4. What do you and your friends like to do on the weekend?
5. What does your son like to do on the weekend?
6. What do you like to do on the weekend?
7. What does your next-door neighbor like to do on the weekend?
8. What does your cousin Sue like to do on the weekend?

Page 10 Exercise N

Listen and write the ordinal number you hear.

Many people live and work in this large apartment building in New York City.

1. There's a barber shop on the second floor.
2. The Wong family lives on the twelfth floor.
3. The Acme Internet Company is on the thirtieth floor.
4. Bob Richards lives on the thirteenth floor.
5. There's a bank on the third floor.
6. There's a dentist's office on the ninth floor.
7. There's a flower shop on the first floor.
8. The Martinez family lives on the nineteenth floor.
9. Louise Lane works on the seventeenth floor.
10. There's a computer store on the fourth floor.
11. There's an expensive French restaurant on the forty-eighth floor.
12. My apartment is on the fifth floor.
13. The Park family lives on the thirty-fourth floor.
14. Dr. Jacobson has an office on the twenty-sixth floor.
15. The Walker family lives on the sixty-second floor.
16. There's a health club on the eighteenth floor.

Page 13 Exercise C

Listen and choose the correct response.

1. Where's the tea?
2. Where are the oranges?
3. Where's the fish?
4. Where are the cookies?
5. Where's the cake?
6. Where's the rice?
7. Where are the pears?
8. Where's the cheese?

Page 15 Exercise F

Listen and put a check under the correct picture.

1. Let's have some pizza!
2. Where are the eggs?
3. Let's make some fresh orange juice!
4. Let's bake a pie!
5. Where are the potatoes?
6. Let's have a sandwich for lunch!

Page 19 Exercise L

Listen and put a check under the correct picture.

1. A. Would you care for some more?
   B. Yes, please. But not too much.
2. A. Do you like them?
   B. Yes, but my doctor says that too many are bad for my health.
3. A. These are wonderful!
   B. I'm glad you like them. I bought them this morning.
4. A. How much did you eat?
   B. I ate too much!
5. A. I bought it this morning, and it's very good. Would you like a little?
   B. Yes, please.
6. A. I really don't like them.
   B. But they're good for you!
7. A. How do you like them?
   B. They're wonderful.
8. A. Would you care for some more?
   B. Yes, please. But not too much.
9. A. Hmm. This is delicious. Would you care for some more?
   B. Yes, please. But just a little.
10. A. This is delicious!
    B. I'm glad you like it. I made it this morning.

Page 22 Exercise C

Listen to the conversations. Put a check under the foods you hear.

1. A. Do we need anything from the supermarket?
   B. Yes. We need a pound of apples, a bunch of bananas, and a head of lettuce.
2. A. What do we need at the supermarket?
   B. We need a pound of cheese, a box of rice, and a bottle of soda.
3. A. Do we need anything from the supermarket?
   B. Yes. We need a loaf of bread, a pound of onions, and a dozen oranges.
4. A. What do we need at the supermarket?
   B. We need a pound of potatoes, a pint of ice

cream, and a jar of mustard.

Page 24 Exercise F

Listen and circle the price you hear.

1. A box of cereal costs a dollar ninety-nine.
2. Two cans cost five dollars.
3. Three jars cost four dollars and seventy-nine cents.
4. It costs twenty-five cents.
5. A bottle costs two forty-seven.
6. Two boxes cost six dollars and sixty cents.
7. Three thirteen?! That's a lot of money!
8. A pound costs a dollar fifty.
9. Two dollars and ten cents?! That's cheap!

Page 27 Exercise M

Listen and choose the correct word to complete the sentence.

1. Add a little . . .
2. Chop up a few . . .
3. Cut up a few . . .
4. Pour in a little . . .
5. Slice a few . . .
6. Mix in a little . . .

Page 29 Exercise E

Listen and circle the correct word.

Ex. I want some lemons.
1. I'd like some ice cream.
2. I need some tomatoes.
3. I'm looking for lettuce.
4. May I have some meatballs?
5. I want some whole wheat bread.

Page 32 Exercise D

Listen and circle the words you hear.

1. I want to have the chocolate ice cream.
2. They won't fax the letter this morning.
3. I want to recommend the fish today.
4. Peter and William won't go home this morning.
5. She won't eat meat.
6. They want to get married soon.
7. He won't buy a car this year.
8. We want to use our computer now.

Page 37 Exercise K

Listen and choose the correct answer.

1. I'm afraid I might get sick!
2. I'm afraid I might fall asleep!
3. I'm afraid I might step on your feet!
4. I'm afraid I might break my leg!
5. I'm afraid I might catch a cold!
6. I'm afraid I might drown.
7. I'm afraid I might get seasick!
8. I'm afraid I might get a sunburn!
9. I'm afraid I might have a terrible time!
10. I'm afraid I might look terrible!

Page 42 Exercise F

Listen and choose the correct words to complete the sentences.

1. A. Yesterday was cool.
   B. I know. But today is . . .
2. A. Ronald is tall.
   B. You're right. But his son Jim is . . .
3. A. This briefcase is very attractive.
   B. Really? I think THAT briefcase is . . .
4. A. Nancy is very nice.
   B. Do you know her sister Sally? She's . . .
5. A. Tom is very fast.
   B. You're right. But his brother John is . . .
6. A. Michael is a very friendly person.
   B. I know. But his wife is . . .
7. A. Your roommate is very interesting.
   B. You're right. But I think YOUR roommate is . .
8. A. The supermarket on Center Street was very busy today.
   B. Yes, I know. But the supermarket on Main Street was . . .

Page 44 Exercise I

Listen and circle the correct answer.

1. Yesterday was hotter than today.
2. The tomatoes are more expensive than the potatoes.
3. Aunt Betty is younger than cousin Jane.
4. Bob is shorter and heavier than Bill.
5. Barry's chair is more comfortable than Larry's chair.
6. The science test was more difficult than the history test.
7. Irene's office is bigger than Eileen's office.
8. Ronald is more capable than Donald.

Page 56 Exercise F

Listen and circle the words you hear.

1. My new chair is much more comfortable than my old chair.
2. Is that the worst city in the country?
3. I want a more energetic president.
4. Don't you have a cheaper one?
5. What was the most important day in your life?
6. Roger is the sloppiest teenager I know.
7. This is the best perfume we have.
8. Sally isn't as lazy as Richard is.
9. You know, I think your dog is meaner than mine.
10. Howard is the most honest person I know.

Page 59 Exercise G

Listen and circle the correct answer.

Ex. Ronald is younger than Fred.
1. Bob is neater than Bill.
2. The chicken is more expensive than the fish.
3. Moscow is warmer than Miami.
4. Herbert is taller than Steven.
5. Patty is more talented than Pam.

Page 63 Exercise D

Look at the map on page 62. Listen and choose the correct answer.

1. Linda was at the hotel on Ninth Avenue. She walked along Ninth Avenue to Elm Street and turned right. She walked up Elm Street to Eighth Avenue and turned right again. She went to a building on the left, between the flower shop and the post office.

2. Roger was at the shoe store on Eighth Avenue. He walked along Eighth Avenue to Oak Street and turned right. He walked down Oak Street and went to a building on the left, across from the parking garage.

3. Mr. and Mrs. Baker were at the book store on Elm Street. They walked up Elm Street to Eighth Avenue and turned right. They walked along Eighth Avenue to a building next to the pet shop and across from the post office.

4. Wanda was at the department store on Ninth Avenue. She walked along Ninth Avenue to Oak Street and turned left. She walked up Oak Street to a building on the right, next to the toy store and across from the library.

5. Alan was at the motel on Oak Street. He walked down Oak Street to Ninth Avenue and turned right. He walked along Ninth Avenue to a place on the left, next to the supermarket and across from the department store.

6. Alice was at the supermarket on Ninth Avenue. She walked along Ninth Avenue to Oak Street and turned left. She walked up Oak Street to Eighth Avenue and turned right. She went to a building on the left, across from the restaurant.

Page 67 Exercise I

Listen and fill in the correct places.

1. David took the Bay Avenue bus and got off at Second Street. He walked up Second Street to Brighton Boulevard and turned right. He walked along Brighton Boulevard to a building on the right, across from the post office. Where did he go?

2. Barbara took the Day Street bus and got off at Second Street. She walked down Second Street to Bay Avenue and turned right. She walked along Bay Avenue to a building between the flower shop and the church. Where did she go?

3. Mr. and Mrs. Jackson took the Bay Avenue bus and got off at First Street. They walked up First Street to Brighton Boulevard and turned left. They walked along Brighton Boulevard to a building on the right, next to the bus station and across from the barber shop. Where did they go?

4. Susan didn't want to take the bus this morning. She was at the library on Bay Avenue. She walked along Bay Avenue to Third Street and turned left. She walked up Third Street to Day Street and turned left again. She walked along Day Street and went to a building on the left, between First Street and Second Street. Where did she go?

5. Mr. and Mrs. Yamamoto wanted to get some exercise this morning. They took the Day Street bus and got off at First Street. They walked down First Street to Brighton Boulevard and turned left. They walked along Brighton Boulevard to Second Street and turned right. They walked down Second Street to Bay Avenue and turned right again. They went to a place on the right, at the corner of First Street and Bay Avenue, next to the concert hall. Where did they go?

6. George got lost this morning. He took the Bay Avenue bus and got off at First Street. He walked up First Street to Brighton Boulevard and turned right. He walked along Brighton Boulevard to Second Street and turned left. He walked up Second Street to Day Street and turned right. He walked along Day Street to Third Street and turned right again. He walked down Third Street to Brighton Boulevard, and then he was happy. He went to a place at the corner of Third Street and Brighton Boulevard, next to the post office and across from the pet shop. Where did he go?

Student Book Thematic Glossary

Actions and Activities

add 24
agree 47
arrive 29
ask 53
bake 13
become 32
begin 29
believe 16
bloom 32
buy 8
call 9
call in sick 36
change 46
chat online 2
chop up 24
clean 5
come 32
come home 44
communicate 8
complain 52
compliment 15
cook 3
cost 21
cut 24
dance 5
decide 23
deliver 27
disagree 47
do 5
draw 69
drink 23
drive 4
drown 35
eat 2
end 29
enjoy 25
fall 34
fall asleep 35
feel 36
fire 43
follow 68
forget 7
get back 60
get home 22
get married 29
get off 66
get out of 30
get to 33
give 6
give advice 8
go 8
go dancing 35
go hiking 2
go out 42
go outside 32

go sailing 35
go skiing 5
go swimming 35
go to bed 22
go to school 36
go to the movies 35
go to work 36
grow up 8
have 13
help 8
hire 43
hope 36
hurry 32
hurt 34
invite 69
keep 27
know 6
lend 8
like 2
listen 9
live 8
look 22
lose 8
make 12
make a list 12
make *pancakes* 4
marry 38
melt 59
miss 46
mix in 24
move 8
name 29
need 20
open 22
order 25
paint 32
pass through 59
plant 4
play 3
play baseball 32
play basketball 2
play tennis 9
play the piano 3
pour in 24
produce 27
put 24
put on 34
read 2
rebuild 59
recommend 23
rent 43
repeat 34
return 29
ride 32
rush 22
say 9

see 31
seem 44
sell 8
send 8
shop 27
sit down 22
skate 5
ski 5
slice 24
spend 16
stand 34
stay home 36
stay indoors 32
step on 35
study 42
suggest 23
swim 3
take 8
take a vacation 8
take a walk 35
take piano lessons 43
take the subway 66
talk 9
taste 17
tell 17
think 6
touch 34
try 44
turn left 64
turn right 64
visit 44
vote 42
wait 31
walk along 63
walk down 62
walk out 16
walk up 62
want 14
watch TV 2
watch videos 4
watch 34
wear 44
wonder 16
work 30
worry 35
write 3

Ailments and Symptoms

cold 32
flu 36
measles 36
nauseous 36
seasick 35
sick 35
spots 36
sunburn 35

Animals, Birds, and Insects

cat 37
dog 40
hen 27
parrot 41
puppy 33

Clothing

blouse 7
boots 32
bracelet 6
clothes 44
earrings 43
evening gown 55
gloves 43
hat 43
jacket 6
jewelry 60
necklace 6
ring 60
sweater 6
wallet 8
watch 6
winter coat 32

Colors

color 33
gray 32
green 32
pink 7
purple 7
red 36

Computers

computer 7
desktop computer 43
e-mail message 9
Internet 8
message 8
notebook computer 43
printer 41

Days of the Week 1

Sunday
Monday
Tuesday
Wednesday
Thursday
Friday
Saturday

Describing with Adjectives

afraid 35
ashamed 52
attractive 41
bad 15

baked 25
beautiful 41
best 54
better 44
big 28
boring 51
bright 50
broiled 25
busy 27
capable 43
careful 34
cheap 42
clean 45
clear 60
close 60
cold 31
comfortable 41
concerned 53
convenient 43
cute 39
delicious 15
dependable 56
different 27
difficult 27
direct 66
disappointed 22
dishonest 59
easy 44
elegant 55
embarrassed 52
energetic 49
enormous 27
excellent 15
exciting 39
expensive 21
famous 31
fancy 40
fantastic 15
fashionable 39
fast 40
favorite 24
first 25
fresh 13
friendly 39
funny 49
fur 43
generous 49
glad 15
good 8
handsome 41
happy 31
hard 44
healthy 44
helpful 49
high 59
honest 42
horrible 52
hospitable 39
hot 39
hungry 22

impatient 59
impolite 59
inexpensive 59
intelligent 39
interesting 41
kind 50
large 27
last 4
late 22
lazy 39
leather 43
left 43
light 28
lightweight 55
little 27
long 27
lost 68
low 27
magnificent 23
mean 49
modern 47
neat 44
new 8
nice 41
noisy 49
obnoxious 49
old 40
out of this world 23
outdoor 60
patient 49
polite 39
popular 49
positive 35
powerful 39
pregnant 36
pretty 40
proud 52
quick 66
quiet 25
ready 30
real 46
reasonable 57
reliable 46
ridiculous 45
right 43
romantic 25
rude 49
sad 32
safe 40
satisfied 44
short 44
sick 9
sloppy 49
small 27
smart 39
soft 39
special 24
spicy 39
stubborn 49
stupid 68

sure 35
sympathetic 44
talented 39
talkative 39
tall 47
tasty 25
terrible 17
tired 22
ugly 52
uncomfortable 59
understanding 44
unfriendly 59
unhealthy 59
unsafe 59
upset 16
used 42
useful 42
wide 47
wonderful 15
worse 56
worst 56
wrong 68

Describing with Adverbs
always 8
completely 68
never 8
often 8
soon 24
usually 28

Entertainment and the Arts
entertainment 60
jazz 5
movie 43
music 44
piano lesson 43
radio talk show 46
rock music 5
TV program 58

Events and Occurrences
anniversary 7
birthday 6
blackout 84
celebration 59
costume party 59
date 25
party 24
picnic 35
vacation 33
wedding anniversary 25

Family Members
aunt 50
brother 30
children 7
cousin 50

daughter 6
family 5
father 4
grandchildren 7
grandfather 51
grandmother 2
husband 6
mother 32
nephew 51
parent 7
sister 50
son 44
uncle 50
wife 6

Food Containers and Quantities
bag 19
bottle 19
bowl 23
box 19
bunch 19
can 19
cup 23
dish 23
dozen 19
gallon 19
glass 23
half a pound 19
half pound 19
head 19
jar 19
loaf 19
order 23
piece 23
pint 19
pound 19
quart 19
slice 27

Foods
appetizer 25
apple pie 13
apple 11
bagel 27
baked chicken 25
baking soda 24
banana 11
bread 11
broiled fish 25
butter 12
cake 11
candy 6
carrot 11
cereal 19
cheese 8
chicken 11
chicken soup 23

chili 27
chocolate bar 27
chocolate cake 15
chocolate ice cream 23
cocoa beans 27
coffee 12
cookie 12
donut 27
egg 11
fish 11
flavor 28
flour 12
food 17
french fries 13
fruit 27
fruitcake 24
grapes 11
hamburger 13
honey 24
hot chocolate 23
hot dog 27
ice cream 12
jam 19
ketchup 11
lemon 11
lemonade 13
lettuce 11
mayonnaise 11
meat 11
meatball 13
meatloaf 41
milk 12
muffin 27
mushroom 24
mustard 11
nut 24
omelet 13
onion 11
orange 8
orange juice 12
pancake 4
pear 11
pepper 11
pizza 13
potato 11
raisin 24
rice 12
roll 28
salad 13
salt 11
sandwich 13
scrambled eggs 23
snack 28
soda 12
soup 19
soy sauce 11
spaghetti 4
stew 24

strawberry 23
sugar 12
Swiss cheese 21
taco 27
tea 12
tomato 11
tomato juice 25
vanilla ice cream 23
vegetable 17
vegetable soup 25
vegetable stew 24
water 24
white bread 19
whole wheat bread 19
yogurt 12

Geography
country 58
desert 59
island 27
mountain 59
ocean 59
river 59
world 27

Getting Around Town
avenue 63
block 68
boulevard 67
directions 68
lane 68
left 62
location 56
right 62
road 68
stop 68
street 46

Home
apartment 33
apartment building 41
appliance 56
bed 22
bedroom 33
cabinet 12
condominium 8
counter 12
dishwasher 40
downstairs 51
freezer 12
furniture 45
garden 32
home 22
house 8
igloo 59
kitchen 12
living room 32
refrigerator 12
rocking chair 41

room 5
rug 40
TV 2
waterbed 59
yard 32

Injuries
break my leg 35
fall 34
get a shock 34
get hit 34
get hurt 34
hurt *your* eyes 34
hurt *your* head 34

Meals
breakfast 13
dessert 13
dinner 13
lunch 13
main course 25
meal 28
menu 25
supper 28

Miscellaneous Nouns
health 15
history 51
idea 36
life 8
location 56
mistake 68
nothing 22
opinion 47
problem 44
pronunciation 45
recommendation 23
size 27
warning 29

Money
cents 21
dollars 16
money 8
price 27

Months of the Year 1
January
February
March
April
May
June
July
August
September
October
November
December

Objects
air 60
amount 27
bag 16
bicycle 6
bookcase 55
briefcase 6
building 47
CD player 7
CD 8
cell phone 40
chair 44
corner 25
costume 59
doll 6
electricity 60
fan 43
fence 32
flowers 4
grass 32
groceries 16
home entertainment
   products 56
ice 59
items 27
letter 5
list 12
location 56
magazine 58
map 69
mixing bowl 24
newspaper 58
novel 45
painting 7
people 31
perfume 6
piano 3
plant 7
polka dots 7
present 6
product 56
radio 54
recipe 24
roller coaster 35
saucepan 24
shopping list 20
story 32
table 25
thing 60
ton 27
toothpaste 53
tree 32
TV 2
video 4
video camera 55
water 60
wig 40
wire 34

world 27

Occupations

actor 58
actress 58
chef 24
dancer 53
doctor 15
landlord 50
mayor 46
professor 43
senator 51
singer 58
teacher 24
TV star 58
waiter 25
waitress 25

Parts of the Body

arm 36
eyes 34
feet 35
hair 44
hand 43
head 34
leg 35

People

boss 45
boy 32
girl 52
guest 30
neighbor 51
people 31
person 50
salespeople 56
student 53
teenager 44
worker 59

Places Around Town

airport 61
amusement park 60
apartment building 41
bakery 28
bank 70
barber shop 62
baseball stadium 61
beach 2
book store 64
bus station 64
bus stop 68
cafeteria 64
church 8
city 47
clinic 62
college 8
concert hall 61
courthouse 61
department store 56
drug store 62

fire station 64
flower shop 61
food store 27
gas station 63
grocery store 27
hardware store 61
high school 8
hospital 8
hotel 59
ice cream shop 61
laundromat 62
library 62
mall 2
motel 61
museum 61
neighborhood 31
office 36
open market 27
park 32
parking garage 61
parking lot 63
pet shop 61
place 27
playground 61
police station 62
post office 62
restaurant 25
school 33
shoe store 61
shopping mall 64
station 59
subway station 59
subway 59
supermarket 16
tourist sight 58
town 56
toy store 61
train station 66
university 61
wholesale store 27
zoo 63

School

class 68
course 43
English class 68
grades 44
history professor 51
student 53
test 31

Seasons 1

spring
summer
fall/autumn
winter

Sports and Recreation

camping 60
football 60

fun 60
game 30
recreation 60
soccer 60
sport 58
sports equipment 60
swimming pool 59
tennis racket 40
walk 32

Time Expressions

a minute 24
all the time 17
all *year* 32
at *7:00* 30
day 1
early in the *evening* 28
evening 25
every day 3
every *morning* 36
for *45* minutes 24
for a long time 27
for many *years* 8
for *three* hours 24
hour 24
in a few hours 30
in a few minutes 30
in a few more *weeks* 32
in a little while 30
in a week 30
in an hour 30
in *five* minutes 30
in half an hour 30
in the past 27
in *two* or *three* days 30
last January/February/
 . . . / December 4
last night 4
last spring/summer/fall
 (autumn)/winter 4
last Sunday/Monday/
 . . . /Saturday 4
last week/weekend/
 month/year 4
month 1
next *Saturday* 33
now 8
on *Sunday* afternoons
 32
on the weekend 2
once or twice a week 27
right now 3
season 1
some day 31
the middle of the
 afternoon 28
these days 27
this January/February/
 . . . /December 5

this morning/afternoon/
 evening 4
this spring/summer/fall
 (autumn)/winter 4
this Sunday/Monday/
 . . . /Saturday 5
this week/weekend/
 month/year 4
time 27
today 4
tomorrow 3
tomorrow morning/
 afternoon/evening/
 night 9
tonight 5
two years ago 6
week 27
weekend 2
year 1
yesterday 3
yesterday morning/
 afternoon/evening 4

Transportation

bus 66
bus system 46
car 42
motorcycle 42
sports car 40
train 30
van 8
wheel 59

Weather

cold 32
cool 47
hot 47
rain 31
rainy 47
snow 32
snowy 47
storm 30
sunny 32
warm 32
weather 32

Work

boss 45
company 27
company picnic 35
helmet 29
job 8
machine 34
office 36
safety glasses 29
work 22

Correlation Key

Student Text Pages	Activity Workbook Pages	Student Text Pages	Activity Workbook Pages
Chapter 1		**Chapter 5**	
2	2	40	40
3	3	41	41–42
4-5	4–7	42–43	43–46
6	8	45	47–49
7	9–11	47	50
Chapter 2		**Chapter 6**	
12	12–13	50	51
13	14–15	51	52–54
14	16–17	54–55	55–57
15	18–20	**Check-Up Test**	**58–59**
Chapter 3		**Chapter 7**	
20	21–23	62	60
21	24	63	61
23	25–26	64-65	62–64
24	27	66	65–66
Check-Up Test	**28–29**	67	67
Chapter 4			
30	30		
31	31–33		
33	34		
34	35		
35	36–39		